Walks & Rambles on the

DELMARVA PENINSULA

A Guide for Hikers and Naturalists

JAY ABERCROMBIE

Backcountry Publications
Woodstock, Vermont

An Invitation to the Reader

If you find that conditions have changed along these walks, please let the author and publisher know so that corrections may be made in future printings. If you wish to be advised of significant trail relocations, or other changes affecting the walking routes mentioned in this guide, send us your name, address, and the title of this book. Address all correspondence to:

Editor
Walks and Rambles Series
Backcountry Publications
P.O. Box 175
Woodstock, VT 05091

Library of Congress Cataloging-in-Publication Data

Abercrombie, Jay, 1942-
  Walks and rambles on the Delmarva Peninsula.
1. Hiking — Delmarva Peninsula — Guide-books.
2. Walking — Delmarva Peninsula — Guide-books.
3. Trails — Delmarva Peninsula — Guide-books.
4. Delmarva Peninsula — Description and travel — Guide-books. I. Title.
GV199.42.D44A33 1985   917.52'1   85-15813
ISBN 0-942440-27-7 (pbk.)

Design by Ann Aspell
Maps and calligraphy by Alex Wallach
Photographs by Reid Jones on pp. 135 and 144; all other photographs by the author

To Marsha, who was there

Contents

DELAWARE BAY/ATLANTIC OCEAN 127

Acknowledgements

During the time required to write this book, I was helped by many people who provided information and encouragement. Most of these people I had met only for the first time, and most were hikers who took a personal interest in making this book a fact.

Although I am grateful to everyone who contributed to the completion of this work, I want to make special mention of the following. Chazz Salkin, Delaware Division of Parks and Recreation, originally conceived the idea of a hiking guide to the Delmarva Peninsula; he made available all his preliminary notes and was always eager to answer questions, provide information, or explore a new trail with me. Noelle Lane, James W. O'Neill, and Cara Wise, also of the Delaware Division of Parks and Recreation, helped me with maps, natural history, and archaeology of Delaware.

All state park managers in Delaware gave complete cooperation during my visits. Special thanks for their personal efforts and hospitality goes to Timothy J. Coffin (Walter S. Carpenter, Jr.), David Cretty (Trap Pond), and Michael J. Felker (Lums Pond). Foresters John C. Bennett and Floyd Simmons helped with Blackbird and Redden State Forests respectively.

In Maryland, Harry Hunter, director of the Office of Recreation and Leisure Services of the Department of Natural Resources, provided information on the Maryland Eastern Shore state parks. Joe Reinhardt, Martinak State Park, shared his considerable knowledge of Indians with me. Stark McLaughlin helped with state forest lands, especially Seth Demonstration Forest. Other Marylanders who assisted include Jay L. Geesman (Pocomoke River State Park), Richard H. Murray (Pocomoke State Forest), Chris Anderson (Tuckahoe State Park), Randy Blass (Wicomico Demonstration Forest), and John Michel (Elk Neck Demonstration Forest).

On the Eastern Shore of Virginia, William L. Allen, Accomack County Parks and Recreation Commission, talked of outdoor recreational opportunities in general and Wallops Park in particular.

Staff members of the U.S. Fish and Wildlife Service cooperated fully during my work on six national wildlife refuges, especially George O'Shea (Prime Hook), Frank Smith (Bombay Hook), Jim Kenyon

ix

(Chincoteague), and Sherman Stairs (Eastern Shore of Virginia). Robbie Sampsell, National Park ranger, helped me explore Assateague Island.

Outdoorsmen on the peninsula were always ready to point out hiking trails and offer advice on good places to walk. Pat Boyle, of the Mason-Dixon Trail System, and Turner Darden, of the Wilmington Trail Club, were especially helpful. Norman G. Wilder and Karen Traverse, Delaware Nature Education Society, were a wealth of information on the natural history of Delmarva. Butch Evans, who operates Old Inlet Bait and Tackle near Indian River Inlet, treated me to tales of living on a dynamic, ever-changing shoreline and of fishing along the coast.

Walking can be more enjoyable in the company of good friends and pleasant companions, and I was fortunate to often share my hikes with Renee Barlow, Helena Tomick, Toni Mattia, and my wife, Marsha, along with my two dogs, Barnacle and Petie.

To my editor, Jane McGraw, and my keyboarders, Gloria Valenza and Jeffrey Patterson, I owe many thanks for their help and patience through numerous revisions. Finally, I would like to acknowledge Reid Jones for taking the photographs on pp. 135 and 144.

Walks & Rambles on the
DELMARVA PENINSULA

Introduction

THE DELMARVA PENINSULA IS A SHARPLY DEFINED piece of land along the Atlantic Coast. Geographically, biologically, historically, culturally, and politically, it is unique among the regions of the United States. Dangling like a cluster of grapes from the mainland, the peninsula is bordered by the Susquehanna River and Chesapeake Bay on the west and by the Delaware River, Delaware Bay, and North Atlantic Ocean on the east. In this book, the northern boundary is arbitrarily defined as the Mason-Dixon Line separating Delaware and Maryland from Pennsylvania. The peninsula narrows at the shoulders but broadens to a wide girth before tapering precipitously to its southernmost point at Cape Charles.

Three states share the small peninsula — Delaware, Maryland, and Virginia — the names combined giving it the name *Delmarva*. The entire state of Delaware lies on the peninsula, occupying about 37 percent of the land area but holding approximately 63 percent of its people. Most of the population is centered around Wilmington in the north. Part of Maryland occupies slightly more than half the land area of the peninsula. Nine counties (from north to south: Cecil, Kent, Queen Anne's, Caroline, Talbot, Dorchester, Wicomico, Worchester, and Somerset) comprise the Maryland Eastern Shore, that part of the state east of the Chesapeake Bay. The Virginia Eastern Shore is small, containing only the counties of Accomack and Northampton.

The Delmarva Peninsula covers a total of 6,485 square miles. It is over 200 miles long and at its greatest width is about 70 miles across. Slightly less than one million people live on Delmarva according to the 1980 census, but the population is unevenly distributed. The vast majority live in the north, particularly in Wilmington, Newark, and Elkton. A smaller urban core is centered around Salisbury near the middle of the peninsula. The ocean resorts of Rehoboth Beach, Bethany Beach, Ocean City, and Chincoteague become crowded with large numbers of tourists in the summer.

Almost the entire peninsula lies within the Coastal Plain, a land noteworthy for its flatness. Here, in the maritimes, you are seldom far from water. Wide, deep tidal rivers indent the Maryland Chesapeake shore. The rivers and the far-spreading marshes tend to isolate towns

1

and communities. It is sometimes shorter to travel by water rather than by road between two points. Even the uplands of the Coastal Plain on Delmarva are frequently swampy. Beginning in Maryland and extending south through Virginia, the mainland lies behind outer, low-profile, barrier islands and shallow bays. Many short streams curl through the marshes on the east side, emptying into Delaware Bay or into one of the small, shallow lagoons.

Most of the hikes in this book are on the Coastal Plain. They reach into virtually every habitat available here: upland oak-pine forests of willow oak, pin oak, post oak, Spanish oak, loblolly pine, Virginia pine, and pitch pine; bottomland swamps of baldcypress, black gum, overcup oak, and red maple; salt marshes; islands bordering the rivers, bays, and ocean; sandy beaches; sand dunes; isolated hilltops; and even man-made environments such as old millponds, a canal, and a historic town.

The Coastal Plain is an area of prosperous farms and small, watermen communities. The peninsula below the northern megalopolis is rural and agrarian. The rich farmland is interspersed with isolated wild areas preserved along marshy creeks or set aside as state parks and forests. Wildlife is abundant and diverse, and plant life is rich and luxuriant, adding a sense of excitement and wonder to almost any hike. Walking is the right tempo for experiencing this land, so often overlooked by car travelers as they speed between home and the ocean beaches.

At the extreme northern edge of Delmarva, the landscape changes dramatically. Here, beyond the fall line, is a small area of low, rolling hills and swift-flowing streams — the Piedmont. Delmarva's highest elevations occur here. The first four hikes in the book (Ashland Nature Center, Brandywine Creek State Park, Bellevue State Park, and Walter S. Carpenter, Jr. State Park) are all in the Piedmont. The walks over this terrain are steeper and more rugged, traversing rich woodlands of oak, hickory, tulip tree, and beech often interspersed by open meadows and old fields.

The biggest cities and heaviest industry occur near the fall line and into the Piedmont, yet some of the best hiking is found here. The gentle hills and rounded valleys offer refreshing variety amid a scenic setting home to chipmunks and red squirrels. On hot summer days, the cool shade of the thick forests provides a welcome environment for a walk.

Most of the Delmarva trails allow you to escape the cares and troubled thoughts of civilization. No matter the season or the weather, you can

2

become immersed in the natural sights and sounds surrounding you. Kingfishers flash from tree to tree along a creek. The true winter call of the blue jay resounds from a tangle of shrubs. Here, at the edge of the woods, birds send whistled messages to each other, warning of your approach. The soft rushing of water, the sighing of wind in the trees, the noise of your own feet on the trail are sounds that, once experienced, will remain with you for a lifetime. Years later, in reverie, you can look at a map and point to one spot or another and immediately be there.

Delmarva lies in a transition zone for vegetation and is at the northern limit for several species of southern plants. Baldcypress, loblolly pine, red bay, and sweetleaf reach their northernmost stands on the peninsula. Other southern species, such as magnolia, sweetgum, pawpaw, mistletoe, holly, and tulip tree, are common. Delmarva also claims a few unique plants of its own. For example, some hybridization among oaks has been found where the coastal species meet the Piedmont species. Seaside alder is endemic to Delaware and the Eastern Shore of Maryland. Unusual nontidal freshwater ponds, called Carolina bays, are found in a small area of the peninsula and contain rare grasses, sedges, and rushes that occur nowhere else in the United States.

Some southern animals, especially invertebrates such as insects and clams, are also at their northern range limits in the region. The peninsula is noted as an important haven for wildlife. The eastern tiger salamander, listed as an endangered species in Maryland, is found only in the Old Line State's Kent County, where it breeds in a few isolated ponds. The rare Delmarva fox squirrel is found nowhere else on earth. Threatened birds of prey, especially bald eagles, ospreys, and peregrine falcons, occur in encouraging numbers here. Waterfowl and wading birds are plentiful. The overwintering populations of ducks, geese, and swans on the peninsula and adjacent waters provide a spectacle of wild America equaled in very few other locations.

Throughout your walks and rambles, you will be aware of the rich historical heritage of this land. Few evidences of the original inhabitants — the Indians — remain, but their influence lives on in the place names of rivers, islands, and bays: Chincoteague, Assateague, Assawoman, Sinepuxent, Chesapeake, Tuckahoe, Pocomoke, Nanticoke, Susquehanna, Choptank, Annemessex, and Indian River. Layered over the ancient Indian civilizations is the more recent heritage of European colonization. Vestiges of Swedish and Dutch colonial days can be found in Delaware, but most of Delmarva has a decidedly English flavor.

3

Names of towns and other governmental jurisdictions reflect this tradition: Sussex, Princess Anne, Queen Anne, Queenstown, Cambridge, Oxford, Centreville, Dover, New Castle, and Royal Oak.

This English heritage permeates most of rural Delmarva south of the urbanized sector. Linguists find that the native accents resemble the English spoken during the Elizabethan age. The area's isolation disappears a little more each day, but the peninsula remains one of the last, truly idiosyncratic parts of the United States, ranking with coastal Maine, southern Louisiana, Texas west of the Pecos, and outlying parts of Hawaii and Alaska. The people are a tough, old-fashioned breed, secure in their convictions and self-sufficient in their ways, content to be left alone but also friendly and helpful. Gilbert Bryon perhaps best described these people's attitude in his poem "The Eastern Shoreman":

> Sure, I've lived here all my life.
> Why turn the world inside-out
> When you're born in paradise?

HOW TO USE THIS BOOK

This trail guide is divided into three geographical areas: The North, Chesapeake Bay, and Delaware Bay/Atlantic Ocean. Each region offers a wide variety of different scenery and unique characteristics, an unexpected surprise for such a relatively small area.

Each chapter provides a complete description of a hike, detailed instructions on how to reach the trail head from a county seat or other nearby large town, and a commentary on the area's natural or human history. A capsule highlight of what can be seen is provided at the beginning of each hike's description, along with the distance and an estimated hiking time. The latter figure is an average that tries to allow for sudden sightings of wildlife, lingering over woodland wild flowers, or moments spent contemplating a grand landscape.

Also listed at the outset is the United States Geological Survey (USGS) 7.5 minute quadrangle map or maps showing the area of the hike. When available, other maps (such as those published by state parks) that show the area or the trails are also mentioned. All these maps are mentioned only to provide the hiker with more detailed information if desired. They are not specifically needed to follow the trails, since sketch maps of each hike are pictured in the book. On these latter maps, the following standard map symbols are used:

parking   ℗

main trail   • • • •

side trail   . . . . .

ferry

point of interest   ■

wharves   ‖‖‖

bridge

tower (observation, radio, water)

There is no need to walk the trails in sequence. Each chapter is designed to stand alone. Simply pick out a hike suitable to your time, circumstances, and interests. Hiking on Delmarva is possible during all four seasons. Most winter days are warm and sunny; snowfalls are generally light and short-lived. Many people find winter the ideal season to be on the trail because they avoid the heat, ticks, and biting insects of summer. Warm weather walks, on the other hand, can be especially scenic and pleasant. Summer is rich with color and activity in nature, while spring and autumn offer the vibrant changes in which all living things become immersed.

THE TRAILS

Some of the hikes in this book are along marked and maintained trails, but most are on paths with no markings and no signs. Still, the majority of the hikes described here are easy and safe. They often follow old forest roads, firebreaks, shorelines, or informal paths blazed by fishermen and hunters, so bushwhacking is seldom necessary. I believe it is impossible to get lost for long in any of the areas described here; civilization is never far away. If you should become temporarily disoriented, take comfort in Bacon's sage advice ("He that follows nature is never lost"), and you will soon come upon a road or water-course.

Two long-distance footpaths in the north are of particular interest to hikers. The Brandywine Trail runs through the Brandywine Valley of Delaware and Pennsylvania. A short segment of this trail that traverses public land is described in the chapter on Brandywine Creek State Park. The Mason-Dixon Trail is a new path that traverses land

5

in the vicinity of the Mason-Dixon Line in Delaware, Maryland, and Pennsylvania. Much of the trail is now on back roads, but volunteers are active in establishing a trail right-of-way in the woods.

All trails in the book except one are day walks and can be classed as easy to moderate in difficulty (even those in the Piedmont). The lone, long, backpacking trip on Assateague Island is a rigorous hike requiring experience, skill, and stamina — a challenge testing your leg muscles and nerve.

BEACH WALKING

Hikers on the Delmarva Peninsula are truly fortunate for the many opportunities for beach walking. Beaches are much more open than the flat woodlands of Delmarva, and you can see for miles along them. William H. Amos has called walking on a wild beach "a splendid isolation that separates you from the rest of the world and returns you to the natural — even primeval earth . . . . It is as though you were the only person in the world, walking upon pristine sands that bear no tread of any living creatures, leaving behind footprints that as surely as the tide rises will soon be erased forever."

Clearly, then, hikes along beaches bordering the ocean, the bays, and the tidal rivers and creeks add a dimension to walking that cannot be gained in forested mountains or rocky hills. All or part of the following hikes in this guide are along a variety of beautiful, often uncrowded, beaches: Elk Neck State Park, New Castle Historic Area, Pea Patch Island, Eastern Neck Island, Janes Island State Park, Cape Henlopen State Park, Delaware Seashore State Park, Fenwick Island State Park, and the backpacking trek on Assateague Island.

Beach walking, however, requires some special preparation and considerations, based largely upon common sense. In the summer, suntan lotion or sunscreen cream, combined with sunglasses and a hat, are necessary to prevent undue exposure to the sun. If barefoot, be careful to avoid sharp shells, rocks, jellyfish, or worse, broken bottles cast up on the shore. (Also, remember to apply suntan lotion to your feet; nothing can ruin an outing faster than sunburned feet.) Carry repellent in your pack in case biting insects become bothersome. Also consider carrying a pair of lightweight sneakers or shower shoes, a swimsuit, and a beach towel.

In spring and early summer, some beaches as well as the dunes just behind the beaches may be nesting areas for shorebirds. Avoid entering

6

these areas, and keep your dog from ranging through the colonies. Birds like terns and skimmers are under great pressure from shore development, off-road vehicles (ORVs), and just the sheer number of people on the beach, and their nesting success in recent years has greatly diminished. They need our help.

Beach walking in cold weather can be especially rewarding because few people are out and you can be truly alone with the sea and the sand. The mild winter days along the Delmarva coast are ideal for hiking. Even quite severe weather should be no hindrance to your walking if you are properly clothed against the chill wind and spume that may blow off the water. Although a winter beach can be astonishingly beautiful, it also can be punishingly cold.

CLOTHING, GEAR, AND OTHER CONSIDERATIONS

Experience will determine the best clothing for your day hikes. I almost always wear hiking boots, even for relatively short hikes, but sneakers are fine for most walks in this book. Wear footgear you do not mind getting wet or muddy. I usually walk barefoot on beaches but carry sneakers in my day pack in case I encounter woodland, brush, or rough terrain. Backpacking always requires boots.

I usually wear shorts in the spring, summer, and autumn. They are much cooler and I can often feel or see ticks as they crawl up my legs. However, some of my hiking friends think long pants tucked into high boots should be worn in tick country. This approach, combined with a special tick repellent, is necessary if you expect to encounter hundreds of ticks — a possible occurrence on the peninsula during certain seasons. Shorts also become a disadvantage when biting insects are numerous, because so much more skin is exposed to their attacks.

I usually carry a light pack for stowing my gear — lunch, water in a plastic bottle (water from Delmarva ponds and streams is unsafe to drink), and perhaps a rain parka or a swimsuit depending on the weather outlook. This guide book is designed to fit easily into your pack; take it with you on the trail. One other very important item for Delmarva walks is insect repellent. A separate little first aid kit containing a few bandages and moleskin for foot blisters is a good idea. From there, you may consider any of the following as appropriate for your pack, depending on the trail and weather: knife, matches, flashlight, compass, space blanket, sunglasses. I also like to carry lightweight binoculars and perhaps a field guide or two to identify flora and fauna. The only poisonous snake recorded on the Delmarva Peninsula is the northern copperhead, but it is considered rare. Count yourself lucky if you see a snake of any species on your walks; I can remember observing only two during my many treks on Delmarva. Like most wild creatures, they scurried away quickly.

A CONSTITUENCY FOR HIKING

The trails of Delaware and the Eastern Shore receive comparatively little use. I met only a handful of hikers on these trails. and I often walked on weekends and holidays — times when the most people should be afield. Seemingly, Delmarva is one of the last areas to be discovered by the walking public. The long-distance trails in the north and the backpacking trail on Assateague Island (Delmarva's only national park) are focal points for hikers, but even these trails are seldom crowded.

A few local resource managers with strong personal interests in walking have provided noteworthy opportunities for varied hikes — the trail networks in Delaware's Walter S. Carpenter, Jr. State Park and in Maryland's Seth Demonstration Forest are two good examples. But all too often the land managers neglect us. The three biggest state parks in the area — Maryland's Tuckahoe and Janes Island, and Delaware's Cape Henlopen — have either no marked trails or a few, short, disconnected nature trails. The seven-mile trail network at Elk Neck State Park is the longest in the Maryland Eastern Shore parks — it was built by the Civilian Conservation Corps in the 1930s. As far as I could determine, no new trails have been added since then. Most of the national wildlife refuges, the type of public land with the greatest acreage on the peninsula, have few footpaths. Perhaps they can be excused because their primary responsibility is to protect wildlife (although shooting blinds are provided for hunters) and because most of their property is on marshland with no solid ground for normal walking. Other public lands provide facilities for just about every other kind of outdoor activity — hunting, fishing, camping, boating, canoeing, swimming, jogging, snowmobiling, four-wheeling, even hot-air ballooning and Frisbee golf. Most of the enthusiasts who practice these sports are organized. They are members of activist groups and are ready to flood land managers, state legislators, congressmen, and senators with letters whenever they get the signal.

8

We need a constituency for hiking. Tell park rangers and managers that you enjoy hiking and would like to see more maintained trails in your nearest park or refuge. Write letters to lawmakers and directors about your interest in hiking and backpacking opportunities. Join and support a hiking club or outdoor organization active in lobbying for funds for new trails, maintenance and enhancement of present trails, and acquisition and protection of land for outdoor recreation.

So much more could be done to improve hiking and backpacking on the peninsula. Scouting groups, trail clubs, or volksmarch clubs could adopt some of the trails featured in this book, providing maintenance, blazes, interpretative signs, etc. Most of the trails I have written about could easily be expanded and linked with other footpaths, creating networks that would add miles and hours of hiking pleasure. In addition, many other areas suitable for walking occur around Delmarva. The opportunities are there; we need merely to take advantage of them.

The following selected clubs and organizations sponsor hikes and other outings (such as backpacks, volksmarches, canoe excursions, and birding trips) on the Delmarva Peninsula. They consist of active volunteers striving to make the environment a better place for people and wildlife.

Brandywine Valley Outing Club
P.O. Box 7033
Wilmington, Delaware 19803

Chesapeake Bay Foundation
162 Prince George Street
Annapolis, Maryland 21401

Committee to Preserve Assateague Island
616 Piccadilly Road
Towson, Maryland 21204

Delaware Nature Education Society
Ashland Nature Center
P.O. Box 700
Hockessin, Delaware 19707

First State Webfooters
% 436 ABG/SSRC
Dover Air Force Base
Dover, Delaware 19902

9

Mason-Dixon Trail System
118 Rustic Drive
Newark, Delaware 19713

Mountain Club of Maryland
14 Solar Circle
Baltimore, Maryland 21234

Tidewater Appalachian Trail Club
P.O. Box 8246
Norfolk, Virginia 23503

Wilmington Trail Club
P.O. Box 1184
Wilmington, Delaware 19899

CONSERVATION

White settlers have lived on the Delmarva Peninsula for over three hundred years. No virgin land remains, except possibly a few acres of remote salt marsh at Bombay Hook National Wildlife Refuge. Hikers are like most outdoorsmen — they develop a deep concern for the air, land, and water so vital to life. It sometimes seems unfair when you return to a favorite woodland where you walked last spring and the area is clearcut, or when a familiar, winding stream is now imprisoned in banks of concrete, or when a wetland is drained. Recently, each year has seen fewer black ducks, striped bass, and marine mammals. Approximately one-fourth of all plant species native to the Delmarva Peninsula have disappeared since 1900. Maryland suffers the highest rate of deforestation of any state east of the Mississippi.

Walking through nature helps us see the interconnectedness of all life. In our efforts to conserve a bit of open space for trails, we encounter problems such as toxic waste disposal, water pollution, water management, acid rain, and multiple use on public lands. Ultimately, every act we take to further conserve our natural resources — by making our own backyard or woodlot hospitable to wildlife, by saving a salt marsh, by improving an antipollution law, by modifying a forest management plan, by increasing appropriations for parks and refuges, by developing a comprehensive energy plan — helps insure that there will be unbroken, undeveloped, wild, and rough places to roam. The trail ahead still harbors unpredictable and refreshing surprises. It still leads us on.

10

The North

Brandywine Creek

Ashland
Nature Center

A pleasant Piedmont walk through farmland and a wooded stream valley

Hiking distance: 2 miles
Hiking time: 1 hour
Map: USGS Kennett Square

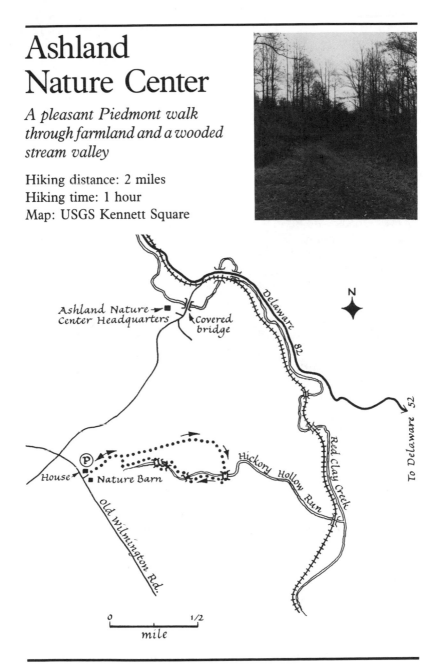

"ENTER THIS WILD WOOD AND VIEW THE HAUNTS of Nature." William Cullen Bryant's invitation could well have been written about this walk through the grounds of Ashland Nature Center in Delaware's gently rolling Piedmont.

Our hike follows an old farm lane past fields and hedgerows to where it ends in a riotous tangle of competing saplings and shrubs. A narrow footpath continues through the thicket, into the woods, and eventually descends to a small, sparkling stream shaded by tall, straight trees a century or more old. Beech, oak, tulip tree, and hickory are the most common trees in this rich bottomland, accompanied by smaller numbers of dogwood, ironwood, spicebush, witch hazel, and red maple. The trail meanders upstream through the little valley, crisscrossing the branch by means of wooden bridges. The clear stream supports a remarkable community living on and in and around it. Water striders, sustained by the thin skin of surface tension on the water, race about the quiet pools. The aquatic stages of caddisflies, mayflies, and stoneflies abound along the bottom, their presence indicating a clean, cool-flowing stream. Crayfish, small minnows, salamanders, and frogs are also common. As the branch grows smaller near its headwaters, the tall trees begin to thin out and the ground becomes muddy and marshy. A few Osage oranges crowd the bank and, in the autumn, drop their fleshy, large, greenish fruits into the stream bed. The path here is narrow and winding, passing through dense thickets of bittersweet, honeysuckle, greenbrier, and blackberry. The trail finally emerges near a marsh and climbs through an old field to link again with the farm lane.

Ashland Nature Center is one of two preserves owned and operated by the Delaware Nature Education Society. (The other is Abbotts Mill near Milford.) The old farm that is the setting for this hike was acquired by the society in 1972. It is extensively used by school groups for classes in outdoor education. The old barn near the parking area has been named the "Nature Barn" and provides introductory programs and services to students and teachers. Emphasis is on the study of biology, geology, ecology, and early human history. Some land is still under cultivation as small garden plots or as agricultural fields.

The Delaware Nature Education Society is an active organization and operates a wide program of nature-oriented activities for all ages. Conducted walks, canoe trips, lectures, films, summer day camps, and excursions to natural areas both nearby and abroad are just some of the programs offered to the public. The staff and volunteers take commonplace natural havens — a gravelly stream bed, a decaying log,

14

a mantid's egg case, a minute snowflake, a giant tulip tree — and help interested individuals intimately inspect them. The headquarters of Ashland Nature Center (about 1½ miles from our trail head) is the nucleus of an extensive trail network that provides more hiking opportunities.

Dogs are permitted if on a leash. I recommend hiking boots for this walk because of the frequently muddy conditions. A fee may be charged to nonmembers for entrance to the grounds.

Many of the programs at Ashland Nature Center are designed to teach children about the plants and animals of Hickory Hollow Run.

ACCESS

Ashland Nature Center is near Hockessin. From downtown Wilmington, drive north on DE 52. After 4.2 miles, turn left (north) onto DE 82. Continue for 3.5 miles, then turn left onto an unnamed road; the intersection is marked with a small sign pointing to Ashland Nature Center. Cross a railroad track, keep left at a fork, cross Red Clay Creek on a one-lane, covered bridge, and come upon the entrance to the headquarters of Ashland Nature Center on the right, 0.2 mile after leaving DE 82. This spot is not our trailhead, but a stop here can be worthwhile. The building contains exhibits and a nature shop and is open daily from 9 to 3 except Sundays and holidays. The grounds and paths are open during all daylight hours. To reach our trail, continue driving, keeping right at a fork, and come upon a stop sign at the intersection with Old Wilmington Road, 1.2 miles from the headquarters. Turn left, go just 0.2 mile, and watch carefully for a driveway on the left marked with a sign saying "School Tours." The driveway is opposite a residential development called Brackenville Woods. Enter the drive, passing between a farmhouse on the left and the white Nature Barn on the right. Beyond, park on the left in a small gravel lot.

TRAIL

Walk straight along the drive, which becomes a farm lane passing between gardens of vegetables and flowers. Continue on the old lane, hiking by fields planted in crops, old fields reverting to natural vegetation, and wood lots. After about two-thirds mile, the lane ends in a grove of young trees and shrubs. Continue straight, walking slightly uphill along a well-worn path.

The trail soon enters a more mature forest and then descends steeply to a small stream, a tributary of Red Clay Creek. A wooden bridge carries you across the branch, dubbed Hickory Hollow Run by the Nature Center staff. On the other side, turn right and walk upstream.

Recross the branch on another small bridge after about one-quarter mile. Walk uphill and turn left on the first side trail. This path soon descends once again into the bottomland. Two more crossings of the stream in quick succession bring you out of the deep forest and into an area of tangled vegetation. Hickory Hollow Run, a small rivulet near its source here, flows slowly beneath the brush. The trail is narrow

16

but clear through this thicket. Occasional boardwalks lift the path out of the mud.

Our trail climbs away from the branch and ascends gently through an old field filled with asters, goldenrods, and small woody plants. After passing through a little clearing, you will come again upon the farm lane. Turn left and walk back to your car.

Brandywine Creek State Park

Magnificent plant life, including unmatched trees and luxuriant wild flowers

Hiking distance: 5½ miles
Hiking time: 3 hours
Maps: USGS Wilmington North; park map

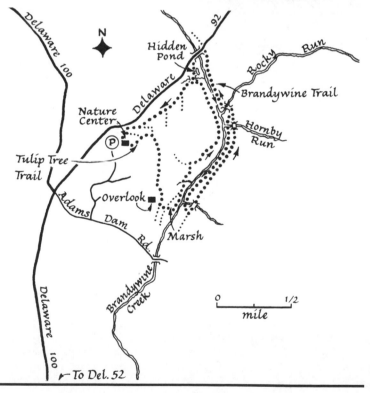

THE PIEDMONT IN DELAWARE IS A HIGHLY SCENIC

land of low, gently rolling hills and fertile valleys. Streams ripple over the countryside, and occasional outcrops of resistant rock indicate that this area is an inland setting, removed both geologically and geographically from the overriding influences of the sea. Only the northern perimeter of Delaware enters the Piedmont; the zone is scarcely ten miles wide at its widest in the state. It is Delaware's most densely populated sector; Wilmington and its suburbs have expanded into the former woods, fields, and farms. The area is characterized by a semi-urban flavor, but the serene beauty of the Piedmont can still be experienced in the remaining open spaces — now the sites of estates, preserves, and parks.

Three of Delaware's ten state parks are in the Piedmont, and the largest of these is Brandywine Creek. The park preserves an especially picturesque section of a valley noted for its scenery, history, and culture. Most of the land in the present-day park was owned from the early 1800s to the 1960s by the du Pont family. The wooded portions of the area have been relatively undisturbed for almost the past two hundred years. The tall trees are spectacular. Albert E. Radford, professor of botany at the University of North Carolina and a leading authority on Piedmont ecosystems, states that "the Brandywine Creek...forest is the most beautiful high-canopied woody community in the entire Piedmont" — a remarkable claim considering the Piedmont covers 85,000 square miles and stretches for 1,000 miles from New Jersey to Alabama. Complementing the forest giants is a rich assortment of wild flowers that color the woodland floor and surrounding meadows each spring. Three hundred species of wild flowers are recorded here.

The great trees are the glory of the park, but a man-made feature also deserves special mention — the artistic stone walls crisscrossing the meadows and forests. They are clearly artifacts — products of civilization — but, being made of earthen materials, they seem to be part of the land and add to the tranquility of the environment. Built a century or more ago by Italians brought to this country to construct the Du Pont Company mills along the Brandywine, they are superb examples of the stonemason's art.

Our trail follows two loops through mature forests, old fields, a floodplain marsh, and riverine habitats, passing by stone fences and a woodland pool to cross Brandywine Creek on a highway bridge. The hike starts at the nature center and initially follows a short segment of the interpretative Tulip Tree Trail. Pamphlets describing the num-

19

bered stations along the way are available in the nature center. Other trails are laid out through the park, but most of these are inconsistently marked and confusing. Follow the directions here and, once off the Tulip Tree Trail, ignore the various-colored trail blazes, signs, and numbers.

ACCESS

From downtown Wilmington, drive north on DE 52 for 2.7 miles. Turn right (north) on DE 100. In 2.4 miles come upon a crossroads where DE 100 turns to the left, DE 92 goes straight, and a side road enters from the right. Turn onto the side road (Adams Dam Road) and drive just 0.2 mile to the entrance of Brandywine Creek State Park on the left. Follow the park road 0.7 mile, always keeping left at forks, until it dead-ends in the nature center parking lot.

TRAIL

Follow the path around the right of the nature center and continue straight through the break in the stone fence onto the Tulip Tree Trail. This path wanders for one-third mile through the 155-acre natural area set aside to protect the majestic trees. At station 7, fork right, leaving the nature trail. You will soon come upon a "T" junction with a broad path; turn right and pass through a wide gap in another stone wall as you leave the forest and enter an expansive picnic area.

The trail continues straight on a former road known as Walnut Lane with an old field, now developing into a young forest, on the left and the grassy, hillside picnic area on the right. Pass a grove of trees on the right. A small spring, surrounded by skunk cabbage, arises from the midst of the grove and flows across the trail.

The lane turns sharply left and then right, descending slightly to an overlook atop an amphibolitic outcrop (elevation two hundred feet) that affords a fine vista of the Brandywine Valley; a marsh bordering the creek is visible immediately below. Turn left off Walnut Lane and follow the trail that zigzags down the rock face to the floodplain below. The rock outcrop is reputed to have been a shelter for Indians traveling along the Brandywine.

At the bottom, cross a broad trail and continue straight on the path through the marsh. (This area floods almost every year; if the way through the marsh is too wet, turn left on the broad trail and join the

20

main trail later.) This marsh differs from the others described in this book. It is freshwater, nontidal, and is home to a host of plants and animals unusual for this region. Cattail, arrowhead, sweet flag, rice cutgrass, giant bulrush, and wild rice occur in the wet interior, while the drier perimeter supports trees and shrubs such as black willow, silver maple, sycamore, and black ash. The secretive bog turtle, a species apparently declining because its habitats are drained and developed, is found here.

Walk across the marsh, come to the bank of the Brandywine, and turn left (upstream). Our trail circles to the left around the head of the marsh and comes out onto the wide trail we crossed earlier at the base of the rock outcrop. Turn right. (If you avoided the marsh earlier because of high water, you will rejoin our main trail here.)

Cross a small stream on a concrete slab, angle left, and pass the ruins of an old springhouse on the left. You will begin a slight ascent, turn sharply left, and, farther up the slope, come upon a junction with a wide trail going both left and right. Other trails junction a few paces to the left. Turn right on the broad path and follow the contour of the slope. The way mostly passes through an old field being invaded by saplings and offers splendid uphill views of old-growth tulip trees. The Brandywine comes back into sight on the right, and the trail continues along the stream bank.

After the path veers to the left away from the creek, a side trail goes off to the right and crosses a ravine on a winding wooden bridge. Follow this side trail for the second loop of today's walk; you will return to this spot later.

Beyond the foot bridge, our path passes by Hidden Pond, a little body of water nestled in a remnant of the old creek bed. A boardwalk on the other side of the quiet pond crosses the bottom and allows hikers to keep their feet dry. The trail again reaches the creek just below Thompson's Bridge. Go around a fence that ends at two giant sycamores and scramble up the steep bank to the road (DE 92). Cross the bridge (built in 1934) and turn right into the parking area on the far side. Walk through the small lot, step around a cable barricade, and continue straight on an old, unpaved roadway known as the Creek Road. White blazes on trees along here indicate you are on the Brandywine Trail, a long-distance hiking path maintained by the Wilmington Trail Club. Running from Wilmington north into Pennsylvania, it largely traverses private lands (at least in Delaware); passage across these sections is restricted to members of the club or to hikers

21

escorted by club members. Here in the park, the Brandywine Trail links with other footpaths open to everyone.

Cross Rocky Run on a bridge and turn right off the old Creek Road, following the white blazes of the Brandywine Trail along the creek bank. The path here is narrow and weaves through the tangle of bottomland growth. Cross Hornby Run. Beyond another, unnamed stream, the Brandywine Trail angles to the left, away from the creek, and climbs gradually to rejoin the former Creek Road. Turn left on the old road (leaving the Brandywine Trail which continues downstream) and hike back to the bridge over Rocky Run. From here, retrace your steps to DE 92, cross Thompson's Bridge, skirt Hidden Pond, and arrive back at the spot where you started the second loop. Turn right.

Climb very gradually out of the creek valley. The trail splits as it emerges from the woods; take the right fork. Keep right also at the next fork, choosing the more level trail that reenters the forest. This path soon narrows and passes through a back section of the natural area. Gigantic trees watch over the land as it must have looked when this country was young. When our path junctions at a "T" with a broad trail, turn right and walk straight until you come upon a low, stone wall. Turn left along the stones, and you will very shortly come upon a break in the wall where the Tulip Tree Trail intersects from the left. Station 15 is placed here. Step through the break and head left across the field to the nature center parking lot.

Bellevue
State Park

*Through the forests and
meadows of a former
du Pont estate*

Hiking distance: 2 miles
Hiking time: 1 hour
Maps: USGS Marcus Hook and
   Wilmington North; park map

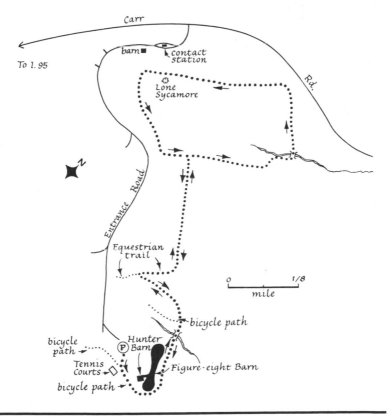

THE NAMES DU PONT AND DELAWARE HAVE BEEN

linked inextricably since 1802 when Eleuthere Irenee du Pont built his black powder mill along Brandywine Creek. The mill began an enterprise that grew into one of the largest industrial concerns in the world. The du Pont family has played active roles in Delaware's industrial, commercial, social, and political circles from that time to the present. For example, Delaware owes many of its museums and its great collections of decorative arts to the philanthropy of the du Ponts. The walk described here also must be counted among the gifts of the du Ponts because it winds around Bellevue, one of the former great estates of the family. Since 1976, when Bellevue became a state park, the forests, fields, and landscaped gardens of the estate have been open to the public.

The Bellevue manor house was constructed in the 1850s, not by the du Ponts, but by Hanson Robinson, a wealthy sea merchant. The cost of construction was $100,000. William du Pont, Sr., purchased the estate in 1893 and added to it over the years. The present appearance of the mansion and the grounds is largely due to the efforts of William du Pont, Jr. He was a dedicated tennis and horse-racing enthusiast and developed a virtually unequaled indoor-outdoor recreational and sporting facility on the estate. Trials for tennis tournaments at Forest Hills and Wimbledon were held here and, in 1943, Bellevue hosted the National Women's Tennis Championships.

But the horse facilities at Bellevue especially catch the attention of today's visitors. A 1⅛-mile race track, an indoor figure-eight riding arena, an indoor galloping track, steeplechase schooling fences, individual stables complete with paddocks, an extensive layout of additional stables, and a horseshoe-shaped formal garden filled with topiary shrubbery depicting riding paraphernalia illustrate William, Jr.'s love of horses and his dedication to the equestrian sports.

Today all areas of Bellevue State Park are available to everyone. As you might guess, most visitors come to play tennis or ride horses. In addition, a fairly extensive network of bicycle trails, incorporating the old race track, is widely used. With the exception of a physical fitness trail with exercise stations, there are no designated paths for the foot traveler. Nevertheless, some of the wooded back acres of Bellevue are well worth exploring on foot, especially during the spring wild flower display. The park contains small but significant remnants of old growth woodlands, an increasingly rare ecosystem in the Piedmont.

The walk I recommend follows bicycle paths and bridle trails into

24

the less-developed portion of the park. Towering black oak, red oak, tulip tree, and sweetgum approach 120 feet in height. The herbaceous ground layer brightens in the spring with jack-in-the-pulpit, trout lily, mayapple, toothworts, spring-beauty, wild geranium, and violets. In the fields and meadows, dandelion, white mustard, and field garlic grow in stands among the grasses.

Most of the horse trails at Bellevue are covered with cinders or wood chips; thus, the hiker usually is spared the churned-up muddy conditions that horses' hooves create. Ticks are found in the fields, so check yourself carefully after the hike.

ACCESS

Bellevue State Park is located on the northeastern perimeter of Wilmington. From downtown, go north 3.9 miles on I-95 to interchange 9, labeled "Delaware 3 — Marsh Road." The exit ramp leads you to Carr Road. Turn left (north) here and continue on Carr Road across Marsh Road. At 0.4 mile from the intersection with Marsh Road, turn right into the park entrance. Drive 0.7 mile to the last parking area ("Mansion Area Parking").

TRAIL

From the parking lot, walk south toward the open tennis courts. Turn left (east) on the paved bicycle path running between the parking lot and the courts. The path leads around the large, figure-eight barn. Today, this barn and the attached hunter barn serve as the park's activity center.

The paved path circles the barn and heads off into the woods in a northwesterly direction, crossing a small stream on a bridge. Soon the paved path veers sharply to the left. Continue straight on a broad, dirt trail, going slightly uphill.

After the trail angles to the left, it intersects a broad, cindered path that is part of the park's equestrian trail network. Turn right and follow the bridle path uphill. At the top of the lane, the trail surface changes to wood chips and the path becomes an old, grand avenue lined with sycamores and maples.

At the end of the lane, a large meadow will appear. Turn right immediately, following a path through the grasses at the edge of the woods. Our trail soon reenters the forest where the path continues

25

along an old stone fence, descending gradually to a small stream. At the stream, turn right and cross the old fence at the base of a gigantic tulip tree. Here, the stone wall vaults the stream, serving as a dam and creating a small pool. Follow the trail downstream until it turns left and crosses the creek on a wooden bridge.

When over the bridge, ascend gradually, leave the woods, and come into a meadow bordering Carr Road. An equestrian trail sign is posted here. From the sign, strike out across the meadow in a southwesterly direction toward a large, lone sycamore, a prominent landmark standing just south of the park's main entrance. At the sycamore, you will pass another horse trail marker and, in the distance behind a barn and at the meadow's edge, you can see another bridle path sign. Walk to this sign and then turn left along the wood fence and the edge of the trees. The park has placed nesting boxes for eastern bluebirds on some of the fence posts along the trail.

Follow the forest-meadow margin for slightly under one-fourth mile as it angles to the left. The entrance to the old, grand avenue upon which you first entered the meadow is visible across the grassy expanse to the left. When across from the entrance, turn left, cross the meadow, and turn right between the rows of trees. Retrace your steps to the parking lot and your car.

Walter S. Carpenter, Jr. State Park

A circuit hike through a park rich in history and scenery

Hiking distance: 5 miles
Hiking time: 2½ hours
Map: USGS Newark West

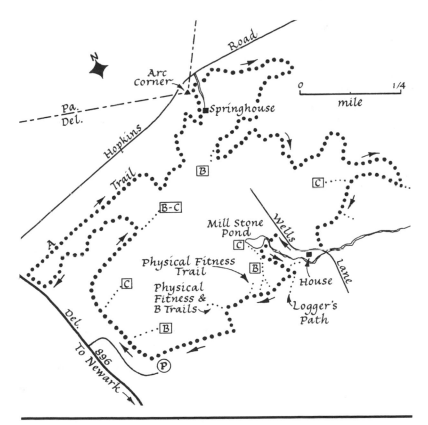

LYING HARD AGAINST THE PENNSYLVANIA BORder, this Piedmont park preserves 436 acres of gently rolling, picturesque hills. Trees grow tall and dense in the wooded portions, but substantial parts of the park are in old fields or grassy areas. Small streams dissect the terrain and flow east into White Clay Creek. Wildlife is varied and abundant; white-tailed deer are so common that hunting is allowed. A large, rocky upthrust (close by our trail) tells of ancient earth movements and is one of the very few such outcroppings found in the state.

The park can also broaden your historical perspectives since it protects significant sites that figured prominently in local history. The rock outcrop was the scene of a small, early-day quarrying operation, providing millstones for a nearby water-powered gristmill. Two incomplete millstones, partially cut out of the rock but never used in the old mill, remain behind.

Boundary disputes among Delaware, Maryland, and Pennsylvania kept the status of this area in doubt for many years. The confusion arose because of inaccuracies in land surveys, mistakes that remained uncorrected even after Charles Mason and Jeremiah Dixon were called in to define Delaware's circular northern boundary and to establish the east-west line marking the border between Maryland and Pennsylvania and the north-south line marking the border between Maryland and Delaware. The arc was supposed to meet the east-west and north-south lines at the same point, but it missed the east-west line by almost one mile. This region became know as the "Wedge". Bandits and other outlaws moved into the area. Using the deep woods as hideouts, they launched raids into neighboring jurisdictions, escaping into the Wedge. The area was also the scene of bloody prize fights as unscrupulous promoters from Philadelphia, sidestepping laws that banned boxing in all three states, staged matches in the disputed Wedge. A compromise that extended the Mason-Dixon Line eastward to intersect the circular boundary gave this land to Delaware in the late nineteenth century. Our trail passes by this point, called Arc Corner.

Walter S. Carpenter, Jr. State Park is a favorite spot for hikers. A trail network consisting of a physical fitness trail, a nature trail, and three separate hiking trails enables walkers to explore virtually all parts of the park. The hiking trails, which lead into the more remote sections, are closed to nonhunters during deer season (generally on selected days of October, November, and January; hunting is never permitted on Sundays). Telephone the park at 302-731-1310 if you have questions.

28

The walk featured here follows the A Trail, the longest of the three hiking trails.

The park commemorates Walter S. Carpenter, Jr., honorary chairman of the board of the Du Pont Company in 1975 when the firm donated about one hundred acres to Delaware as an addition to the then White Clay Creek State Park. State officials changed the name of the park in appreciation to Carpenter and the company. Subsequent donations by Du Pont have created the White Clay Creek Preserve, a natural area that, along with the state park, protects almost the entire upper White Clay Creek watershed.

ACCESS

Drive north on DE 896 from Newark for 2.7 miles. Turn right into the park, continue for 0.2 mile to the large parking area, and leave your car along the left side. The entrance to the trail network is shown by a large wooden map.

TRAIL

The A Trail is well marked by yellow blazes or arrows. Walk northwest on the broad lane, descending slightly. The trail angles to the right as it climbs the opposite slope, then turns sharply left to descend as the B and C trails continue straight and level. Our broad path angles left again as it enters an old field now being overgrown with wild roses, Japanese honeysuckle, Virginia creeper, blackberries, and multitudinous young trees. The fragrant roses and honeysuckles are in bloom in late May and early June. Many birds and small mammals make their homes in this thicket. After some twists and turns, the way reaches DE 896 and curves sharply right for a short distance before veering sharply right again, leaving the highway behind.

Good views of the low, rolling hills await as you descend gradually. Private land, sometimes wooded and sometimes cleared for crops, borders the trail on the left. After a slight ascent, the path turns left to enter the forest and soon passes through a small grove of spruce. Skirt another parcel of private land, with an apparently abandoned house surrounded by fallow fields. The opening affords fine vistas northward into Pennsylvania. Reenter the woods, angle left at each of two successive turns, and descend rather steeply on a broad path. A springhouse can be seen on the right. Continue downhill, paralleling the little run arising from the spring, and come upon a small meadow.

29

The A Trail turns right here to cross the branch, but, visible a few feet ahead in the clearing, is a stone obelisk about five feet high — the monument marking Arc Corner and Delaware's border with Pennsylvania. Bearing the date "1892" and the names of commissioners from both states, the stone is the easternmost marker along the Mason-Dixon Line. (The western end is more than 250 miles from here, near the Ohio River.) Arching northeastward from this point is the circular

The rocky outcrop in Walter S. Carpenter, Jr. State Park is a focal point for Delaware geologists.

boundary between Delaware and Pennsylvania, drawn using the Court House spire in New Castle as the center of the twelve-mile radius (see chapter 8). The road on the far side of the meadow is Hopkins Road.

To continue, follow the A Trail as it reenters the woods and narrows to a single-file footpath. Pass through a dense grove of large white pines, climbing gradually and switchbacking up the slope. Poison ivy is prevalent along the trail. Turn left and follow an old woods road where the white-blazed B Trail enters from straight ahead. The two trails run along together for the next couple of miles.

Pass the crumbling ruins of an old homestead, believed to date from Civil War times. Vines and other woody plants have almost completely swallowed the site, but in the tangle of forest growth you can trace the rough lines of a moss-covered, stone foundation. Embedded in the rocks are chips of shiny mica and orange-colored feldspar, along with larger veins of whitish quartz.

Beyond the ruins, cross two intermittent streams and pass a side trail to the left leading to the park boundary. Later, trails A and B turn left and the C Trail enters from straight ahead to join them. Our way goes through a small tract of pines before emerging onto a broad, mowed path in an old field, now largely overgrown with small trees. As the trail loops to the right, a side path going to the park boundary junctions to the left. Climb gradually but steadily through an old field for about one-fourth mile.

Our trail turns left and descends slightly, narrowing as it reenters the deep forest to cross a hillside high above a little stream on the left. Old beech trees dominate this rich, wooded, south-facing slope. The stream flows into White Clay Creek and comes from a former millpond you will soon reach. You will come out onto Wells Lane, a dirt road, where it crosses the small creek on a plank bridge. Turn right and follow the road uphill.

After passing a house on the left, turn left off the road into a field, following a lane blocked by a chain strung between two posts. The trail passes below an earthen dam impounding Mill Stone Pond. The small pond, surrounded by aquatic vegetation and home to water snakes, frogs, fish, and myriad insects, is near the headwaters of the little stream we saw earlier. It evidently served as a millpond in years past, because the rocky upthrust overlooking the water has two un-finished millstones partially cut from the surrounding rock. The hard schist with veins of gneiss would make ideal millstones for grinding grain.

Just beyond the pond, the A Trail leaves the B and C trails and turns left to follow a broad, mowed swath along the edge of an old field. Fork right and come upon the beginning of the Logger's Path, an interpretative trail, at the edge of the woods. The A Trail turns right here and runs along the margin of the forest, ascending slightly. In a short distance, you will come upon a "T" intersection with a cross trail. Jog left, climb a short, steep bank, then turn right and walk along the edge of the Frisbee golf course. First the B Trail and then the physical fitness trail come in from the right to join the A Trail along the golf course.

Pass through a hedgerow and turn left, uphill. (The B Trail and the exercise trail jog right here before going straight.) You will come upon another hedgerow at the top of the rise; turn right and follow it back to the trail head.

Elk Neck Demonstration Forest

A circuit hike featuring game food plots, an old beaver dam, and a wildlife pond

Hiking distance: 3¾ miles
Hiking time: 2 hours
Maps: USGS North East; forest map

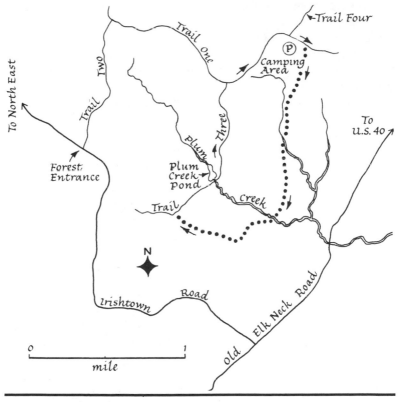

THE DRY, SANDY SOIL OF ELK NECK, A LARGE, wedge-shaped peninsula near the head of the Chesapeake Bay, dictates the types of plant-animal communities existing there and the management trends in land use. The arid uplands support slow-growing, stunted trees. In the past, frequent fires on the peninsula further depleted the soil and resulted in even poorer quality tree growth. In an effort to preserve the environment and to demonstrate modern forestry practices, the state of Maryland began acquiring parcels of land in the late 1930s. Today's result is the 3,165-acre Elk Neck Demonstration Forest. Formerly classified as a state forest, Elk Neck's status was changed in 1983 when it became Maryland's largest demonstration forest. It joined other tracts of state-owned forestland where the management emphasis is on demonstrating scientific forestry for use on private woodlots.

The state protects the young trees in their fragile, upland habitats and also preserves many fine stands of larger trees on the lower slopes and along the streams. The bottomlands, by and large, have escaped the influence of fires. The forest environment needs protection from wanton abuse because mining interests, attracted by the sand and the accompanying large, underlying deposits of gravel, have opened several large sand and gravel pits outside the demonstration forest boundary. The demonstration forest is a reserve where tree scientists experiment with hybrid species to improve timber growth and where hikers and other outdoorsmen explore the woodlands. Elk Neck is a good place to practice your skills in identifying animal tracks; the soft, sandy soils along the trail provide a clear record of the passage of many forest animals.

The hike featured here circles the Plum Creek watershed, but also crosses some upland areas where drier forests can be observed. About half of the hike utilizes hunter access trails, used mainly by sportsmen during legal open seasons in their quest for white-tailed deer, squirrels, rabbits, bobwhite, and mourning doves. Consequently, this hike is not recommended during hunting season. Part of the walk traverses gravel roads that provide access to several primitive camping areas; vehicular traffic is light and rarely encountered. A few ticks and mosquitoes may be found along the brushy sections of the path. The trail I recommend is but one of a number of hikes that can be enjoyed on the hunter access trails, fire breaks, and gravel roads weaving through the forest. Use this hike as an introduction to Elk Neck and then explore further on your own.

ACCESS

From Elkton, go west on U.S. 40 for 1.8 miles and then turn left (south) on Old Elk Neck Road. Drive for 3.9 miles to Irishtown Road and turn right (northwest). After 2.3 miles, the main entrance to Elk Neck Demonstration Forest appears on the right. Turn and proceed along gravel Forest Trail 2 for 0.9 mile. Turn right (east) on Forest Trail 1. Drive past Forest Trail 3 on the right at 0.9 mile, Forest Trail 4 on the left at 1.5 miles and arrive at camping area 1C on the right at 1.6 miles. Turn into the campsite and park.

TRAIL

From the camping area, continue east on foot along Forest Trail 1 for about one-quarter mile. Turn right at the first opportunity on a broad trail blocked against vehicular access by a steel cable strung between wooden posts. In addition to the cable, the posts support sizable colonies of termites. Just after turning off the gravel road, a depression that appears to be the dried-up remnants of an old pond is seen on the left. The trail is a broad swath through an adolescent forest of sweetgum, sassafras, red maple, pitch and scrub pine, and scarlet, white, willow, and chestnut oak.

The dense undergrowth on either side of the trail consists of blueberries, grapes, mountain laurel, and occasional chestnut shoots growing from old stumps. Chestnuts once dominated dry forests throughout eastern North America but are now represented only by small sprouts springing from the insistent roots. Attacked by a fungal disease imported accidentally from Asia at the turn of the century, virtually every American chestnut tree died in less than twenty-five years. This event was an ecological disaster of immense magnitude. Now, almost eighty years after the epidemic spread through the forests, the chestnuts of Elk Neck and elsewhere in the East are still struggling against total extinction. Shoots along the trail stand six to seven feet tall and flower in June; a few may even produce nuts in the autumn. The sprouts may be expected to live about twenty years and reach fifteen feet or so before their bark shatters from the fungus and the tree becomes girdled and dies.

An overgrown side trail angles in from the right about one-half mile from the road. Keep left. Just beyond this junction, note the game food plot on the right. This and other small areas throughout the forest have been cleared and planted with grass, clover, wheat, and fruit-bearing shrubs as food for wildlife.

The path narrows beyond the game food plot and, at times, undergrowth almost blocks the way. At one mile into the hike, you will come to the margin of a wet meadow studded with the trunks and snags of dead trees. This small wetland is at an early stage of succession — moisture-loving grasses and other plants are reclaiming land once flooded by beavers. The dead trees eventually will fall, decay, and become part of the rich humus that will support seedlings of sun-loving trees. Gradually, over the years, saplings of the forest's dominant species will replace these pioneer trees and reestablish themselves in a typical climax community — provided the beavers do not return. A stream, one of the tributaries of Plum Creek, meanders through the meadow, seeking its old bed or simply carving a new one. Forest rangers have placed wood duck nesting boxes on some of the dead trunks.

Continue straight along the margin of the meadow to the old beaver dam — now ruptured — and cross the small stream below the dam. Apparently the beavers are constructing a new pond downstream from this old one. Continue straight, ascending slightly as you hike out of the lowland along a broad, deeply cut trail. Old trunks of poplars, felled by beavers, crisscross the path and make walking difficult. Make your way as best you can; the trail soon comes out of the ravine and gradually levels as it passes through a densely vegetated section, the brushy undergrowth again threatening the path.

At 1¼ miles, pass through another game food plot. This one is dotted with young saplings of black locust, poplars, and scrub pine. Reenter the woods and soon descend slightly to cross Plum Creek, a gravel-bedded stream whose water is attractively stained from organic matter. Beyond the creek, climb gradually for three-fourths mile on a broad path, coming out onto Forest Trail 3, a gravel road. Turn right, downhill.

Near the bottom of the hill, just before Forest Trail 3 reaches Plum Creek Pond, a research plantation on the left marks one of the foresters' efforts to improve timber production on Elk Neck by planting hybrid trees (loblolly pine crossed with pitch pine). Forest Trail 3 crosses the earthen dam impounding the five-acre pond (set aside as a wildlife sanctuary) and then climbs steeply, passing camping areas 3C, 3B, and 3A, respectively.

36

About three-fourths mile from the pond, you will come upon a "T" junction with Forest Trail 1. Turn right, pass camping area 1B and Forest Trail 4 on the left, and arrive back at camping area 1C where you parked your vehicle.

Elk Neck
State Park

*Upland forests surrounding a
tidal marsh and a beach*

Hiking distance: 2¼ miles
Hiking time: 1½ hours
Maps: USGS Earleville; park trail
 system map

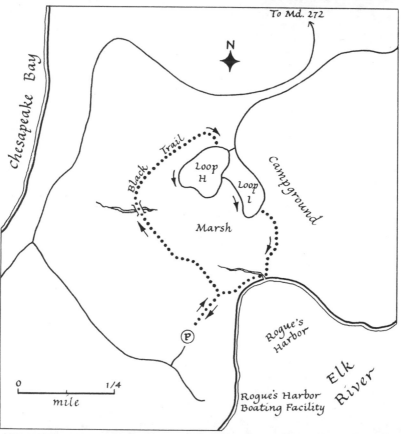

ELK NECK STATE PARK WAS ESTABLISHED IN 1936

when outdoor recreational areas were being developed by the Civilian Conservation Corps (CCC). The trails, roads, picnic areas, and cabins constructed under the CCC program are still enjoyed by visitors today. Largely because of the CCC effort, Elk Neck features five different hiking trails (including a nature trail) totaling over seven miles — more than any other Maryland park on the Eastern Shore. The marked and maintained paths enable hikers to explore the varied topography of the peninsula, ranging from high bluffs overlooking the Northeast and Elk rivers to sandy beaches and from marshlands to mature upland forests.

Wildlife is abundant because of the environmental diversity. Uncommon birds such as wild turkey and great black-backed gull are found here, along with many kinds of songbirds and waterfowl. White-tailed deer, beaver, eastern gray squirrel, and eastern box turtle abound.

Elk Neck is also one of the few Maryland parks that allows dogs. Certain areas, including some trails, are off limits to dogs, but generally you are both free to roam about. Most of the hike described here traverses the Black Trail, one of the longest in the park, so-called because it is marked with black arrows placed on wooden posts. Dogs are allowed on this path. The trailway is easy to find and follow, even though many of the markers have been vandalized.

ACCESS

From Elkton, go west on U.S. 40 for 1.8 miles and then turn left (south) on Old Elk Neck Road. Drive 8.3 miles to a "T" junction with Elk River Lane in the little hamlet of Elk Neck. There, turn right, and then left again immediately at a stop sign onto MD 272 (south). After 2.1 miles, you will enter Elk Neck State Park. Proceed for 2.0 more miles and turn left into the Rogue's Harbor Boating Facility. (If the road to the boating facility is closed, you can park on the right shoulder opposite the entrance and walk to the trail head.) When past the entrance booth, drive an additional 0.4 mile to a large parking lot on the left. Park your vehicle at the back of the lot, away from the sailboat masting area.

TRAIL

At the far end of the parking lot, enter a grassy trail just to the left of a steep gully lined with stone. After about five hundred feet, you will come upon the Black Trail, going to the left and also going straight ahead down a steep, short bank to a beach on the Elk River. No markers are here, but the trail is obvious. Turn left.

The path is thickly surrounded by blueberry; the marsh the Black Trail encircles is visible through the trees on the right. Descend steeply into a weedy bottomland that leads into the marsh. A beaver lodge is located near the shore and signs of tree cutting by beavers are evident in the lowland. Arrowheads, yellow iris, and other aquatic plants can be seen near the shore and in the shallow water. Park rangers have placed wood duck nesting boxes on wooden posts throughout the marsh. Each pole is surrounding by an inverted metal cone placed beneath the boxes to keep out marauding raccoons and other predators. The effort has evidently paid off because the marsh is a favored place to observe wood ducks. In May, mother ducks followed by broods of tiny ducklings can be seen paddling and diving about the aquatic vegetation.

The trail climbs out of the bottom and affords fine views of the marsh at the top of the rise. The path then descends and ascends in turn through two more lowland areas. These rich bottomlands are carpeted with ferns with imaginative and lyrical names: sensitive, cinnamon, lady, and marsh.

Our trail eventually descends into a broad, ferny lowland laced by a small creek feeding the marsh. Cross the watercourse on a wooden bridge and soon climb a long, steep bank into an upland forest. Tulip tree, American holly, mountain laurel, oaks, beech, dogwood, and sweetgum are some of the trees and shrubs bordering the trail.

After crossing a muddy area on logs, the path comes onto loop H of the park's campground. To continue on the Black Trail, turn right on the paved road and walk through the camping area. Turn right at the first opportunity onto another paved road (loop I) and continue to a spot opposite campsite 13. Here, turn right, off the road and onto a trail entering the woods. No marker is placed at this juncture, but a post with a black arrow is soon sighted just before the path begins a gradual descent. Our trail passes through a fine stand of tall pawpaw near the bottom of the hill and then comes out onto a beach on the Elk River.

The beach is a curving, sandy bar separating the marsh from Rogue's (or Rogues) Harbor, a cove of the Elk. A meandering stream flows from the marsh, across the bar, and into the cove near where the trail comes into the open. The stream can be easily leaped when the tide

Elk Neck State Park affords a wide variety of terrain, including a crescent beach.

is out. If you are here at high tide, be prepared to wade the creek or to go upstream where the water breaks out of the reeds; there you can scramble across on piles of driftwood.

Walk along the crescent-shaped beach. Eastern kingbirds and tree and bank swallows are abundant here in the warmer months, busily catching insects on the wing. Scattered about your feet are picturesque samples of driftwood and multitudinous shells of wedge rangia, a brackish water clam at the northern limit of its range. Waves off the shallow cove usually break gently on the shore; it is a welcome place to pull off your boots and socks and go wading — or even swimming.

41

If you tarry long enough, you are bound to see one or two ocean vessels far out in the Elk River Channel sailing to or from the Chesapeake and Delaware Canal.

When you are ready to continue hiking, proceed to the other end of the beach, climb the trail through shrubby vegetation, and arrive at the spot where you first picked up the Black Trail. Retrace your steps along the short spur to the parking lot.

Iron Hill

An enigmatic hill rich in geological, archaeological, and historical lore

Hiking distance: 2 miles
Hiking time: 1 hour
Map: USGS Newark West

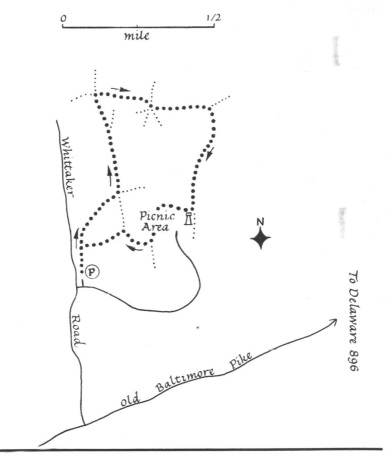

WHEN WALKING THE SLOPES OF IRON HILL, YOU
follow the ancient footsteps of prehistoric Indians who came here to
mine jasper for their stone tools and weapons. You will also cross the
paths of eighteenth- and nineteenth-century miners who opened small,
primitive shafts and pits in the hillside to extract iron ore. From the
tower near the summit, you can imagine how American rebels used
the hill during the Revolution to spy on British troop movements.

The story of Iron Hill begins in a distant geological age. Its origins
are dim and not fully understood by scientists. Today, it is a strikingly
prominent topographic feature, visible from afar. Iron Hill, together
with Chestnut Hill, its slightly lower neighbor to the northwest, forms
an island of gabbro (a granular, igneous rock) surrounded by the sandy
sediments of the Coastal Plain. It is the highest point south of the
Piedmont on the Delmarva Peninsula. The hill's summit stretches to
320 feet above sea level, but it appears higher, especially when viewed
from the east where its hulking, steep slopes tower 270 feet above the
surrounding plain.

Early man was attracted to the hill, perhaps for spiritual reasons
due to its unusual features, and certainly because of the presence of
jasper. Archaeological sites show that prehistoric Indians conducted a
rather sizable quarrying operation on the southwest flank of the hill,
chipping out jasper blocks with stone tools of gabbro and then fashion-
ing the jasper into projectile points, knives, choppers, scrapers, drills,
and other flaked tools.

The ancient Indian quarries were largely obliterated in the 1700s
and 1800s by white settlers looking for another mineral they regarded
more highly than jasper. Welshmen from Pennsylvania, aware of the
reputed reserves of iron ore on the hill, opened the first, small mine
shafts after being granted this tract of land by William Penn in 1701.
So, the hill became known as Iron Hill, the name still used, and for
about the next two hundred years miners broke out chunks of iron
ore with sledge hammers, loaded it into cable cars and wagons, and
carried it to small furnaces where it was converted into steel implements
and weapons.

Mining was not continuous during this period, but flourished or
waned depending upon economic conditions. The last open pits were
operated by George F. Whittaker from 1862 to 1884. The exploitation
of richer iron deposits in the Midwest, coupled with the development
of the modern blast furnace, caused the demise of small, marginal
mines as on Iron Hill. Today, the mining scars are softened by large

44

trees and other vegetation, but you can still discover weathered remnants of iron ore in the old pits pocketing the hillside.

Iron Hill also played a small role in the American Revolution. In August, 1777, a party led by General George Washington, and including General Nathanial Greene and the Marquis de Lafayette, rode to the crest of the hill to reconnoiter British troop movements. The British were planning to mount an attack against Philadelphia, the metropolis of English America and the rebel capital, by sailing up the Chesapeake Bay, disembarking their troops near the head of the bay, and then marching quickly into Pennsylvania to capture the city. Washington and his men sighted only a few enemy tents along the Elk River in Maryland before a severe summer storm forced them from the crest and into a nearby farmhouse where they sought shelter for the night. The storm was an ominous beginning to a bleak period for the American cause. Philadelphia fell to the English the following month and Washington moved his army into a watchful encampment at Valley Forge for the winter.

Most of this hike traverses Iron Hill Park, part of the New Castle County park system. The trail begins near the base of the hill, follows a circuitous route through the woods to an observation tower near the summit, and then descends to the starting point.

ACCESS

From the center of Newark, go south 3.2 miles on DE 896. Iron Hill comes into view on the right as you pass through Newark's southern outskirts and cross the Christina River and I-95 (the Delaware Turnpike). South of I-95, DE 896 runs along the eastern flank of the hill. At the first intersection beyond I-95, turn right (southwest) onto Old Baltimore Pike. This junction is marked with a traffic signal but not a road sign. Old Baltimore Pike follows the old post road, established in 1666, that connected Baltimore with Philadelphia. In 0.9 mile, pass the Iron Hill Museum on the right. Continue for 0.1 mile further and turn right (north) on Whittaker Road. At this intersection, a large sign pointing right shows the way to Iron Hill Park. Whittaker Road takes it name from Whittaker, the miner, who worked on the hill in the late 1800s. Proceed 0.4 mile and turn right into Iron Hill Park. A small parking area is seen immediately on the right. Just beyond, turn left onto a road leading to a larger parking lot and leave your car.

TRAIL

At the end of the lot, go around a vehicle barricade and walk uphill on a broad, gravel service road. In about three hundred feet, a side trail descends from the right; this path will be your return loop. For now, keep straight on the service road.

After about one-fourth mile, turn left off the service road onto a broad, dirt trail. This path leads shortly to an extensive bank of mine tailings on the right. The mound is covered with large trees and Christmas ferns. The forest throughout this section has seemingly experienced relatively little disturbance in recent years. Oaks, hickories, and beech tower to great heights with comparatively little understory. Beyond the mound of mine tailings, the trail narrows to a single-file footpath. At about one-fourth mile from the service road, the woodland trail forks at the head of a ravine. Take the left fork, downhill, following the side of the ravine.

Continue downhill until you come upon a cross trail and, there, turn right. The sound of vehicular traffic from I-95 can be heard in this area. Our trail soon angles left onto an old woods road near where high piles of rock and dirt mark extensive mining activity. Some mounds, now tree-covered, are thirty feet high. This is a good place to look for rusty red, pitted rocks of iron ore on the trail and on the steep mounds.

Just beyond the piles of mine tailings, you will come upon a multi-junction of woodland paths. Use caution here in selecting the correct trail. First, turn right, avoiding the broad trail to the left that descends steeply. Immediately thereafter, the trail forks, with both forks going uphill. Take the left fork. Again immediately, a cross trail is encountered; turn left onto it and continue along a more-or-less level woodland path in an easterly direction.

Proceed for about one-fourth mile, at which point, a well-defined side trail enters from the right. Beyond, the trail we are on veers slightly left and descends. Turn right onto the side trail, proceed uphill, and climb steadily to near the summit of Iron Hill. Here you will come upon the end of a high, chain-link fence separating private property on Iron Hill Road from park property. Keeping the fence on your left, walk along it until you come to a clearing and, there, visible on the right, is the Iron Hill observation tower. The tower is open to visitors Monday through Friday during normal business hours and on some holidays.

At the base of the tower, take the paved path to the right, walk along the head of the summit parking area, and follow the walkway into the picnic area. Keep on the paved path until it ends near the back of the picnic area at a play sculpture. There, turn left and follow the broad dirt trail that leads into the forest.

Shortly, a narrow trail forks left. Keep to the right on the broad trail. Soon another trail intersects at an angle from the left. Turn left here and follow this trail downhill to where it enters the service road on which you began this hike. Turn left and descend to the parking lot.

New Castle Historic Area

A stroll through Delaware's colonial capital

Hiking distance: 1¼–1¾ miles,
   depending on side trail
Hiking time: 1 hour plus
Map: USGS Wilmington South

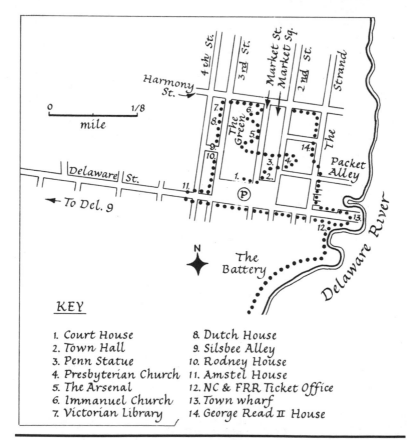

KEY

1. Court House
2. Town Hall
3. Penn Statue
4. Presbyterian Church
5. The Arsenal
6. Immanuel Church
7. Victorian Library
8. Dutch House
9. Silsbee Alley
10. Rodney House
11. Amstel House
12. NC & FRR Ticket Office
13. Town wharf
14. George Read II House

MANY SMALL CITIES AND TOWNS OF DELAWARE

and the Eastern Shore — Dover, New Castle, Saint Michaels, Oxford, Wilmington, Tangier, Arden, and others — have historic districts, open spaces, and unique flavors well worth discovering. New Castle, Delaware, is a prime example. It is an authentic colonial town, complete with eighteenth-century homes still inhabited, some cobblestone streets that have not been asphalted, an ancient church or two with well-kept graveyards, a workable town plan from the 1600s that has been lovingly and proudly preserved, and public buildings associated with the early patriots of our country. The piquant fragrance of two hundred-year-old boxwood hovers along the shady side streets. To add even further to its appeal, New Castle is a place largely undiscovered by tourists.

New Castle owes its present-day appearance mainly to the happenstances of history. The town served as the British colonial capital of Delaware from 1704 to 1776. When the Revolutionary War broke out, New Castle became the capital of the new state of Delaware. But the government was forced to flee inland to Dover in 1777 when British warships on the Delaware River captured John McKinly (the "President of Delaware State") and threatened the town. With the fall of Philadelphia and with the British armada in full control of the Delaware River, New Castle was isolated. The state government never returned. After the war, New Castle maintained some of its prominence by serving as a trade center and as the county seat of New Castle County, but it largely escaped the menace of human negligence and uncontrolled urban expansion of the nineteenth century. By the late 1800s, New Castle had been eclipsed by burgeoning Wilmington to the north, and the county government moved to the larger city in 1881. Left on the sidelines again, New Castle missed the urban upheavals of rapid growth that characterized the first part of the twentieth century. Thus, the downtown area of today's New Castle looks much as it did over two hundred years ago. There are automobiles, utility poles, and other modern accoutrements, but I suspect that many figures from the 1700s would still recognize New Castle if they could visit the town today.

New Castle traces its beginning to 1651 when Dutch colonists built Fort Casimir on the site. The Dutch settlement was an effort to counter Swedish excursions into territory Holland claimed in the early 1600s as a result of Henry Hudson's exploration of the Delaware River. In 1654, Swedes from Fort Christina (today's Wilmington) captured Fort Casimir and renamed it Fort Trefaldighet. The Dutch returned in force the following year, recaptured the fort, and named it New Amstel.

49

They turned New Amstel into a bastion, the southern outpost of New Netherlands in North America. Pieter Stuyvesant, director-general of New Netherlands and headquartered in New Amsterdam (today's New York), came to New Amstel and laid out the town streets and The Green (the central market place) in 1655. Dutch rule was short-lived, however, for in 1664 England captured all of Holland's holdings in North America; after overpowering Stuyvesant's colony of New Amsterdam, Sir Robert Carr led the expedition against New Amstel. The settlement was placed under the rule of the Duke of York (later King James II) and became New Castle. The Dutch regained control briefly in 1673-1674 during the Anglo-Dutch War, but New Castle was returned to the English by the Treaty of Westminster in 1674 in exchange for British islands in the Pacific.

New Castle remained British for over one hundred years, so most of the heritage seen by today's visitor is basically English. In 1682, William Penn arrived in the New World at New Castle and took possession of the vast land grant given to him by the Duke of York. In addition to what became known as Pennsylvania, New Castle itself was specifically deeded to Penn, along with surrounding land extending to a twelve-mile circular boundary. Penn's rule proved capable, and New Castle prospered despite disputes with Lord Baltimore in neighboring Maryland. Friction eventually developed as well with Penn's central colony, Pennsylvania, and Delaware demanded its own home government. Penn reluctantly agreed and granted a separate assembly to the Three Lower Counties On Delaware in 1704. Delaware was born and New Castle was named the capital.

Our walk begins and ends at the Court House, weaves through the heart of the historic area, and includes an optional spur through a riverside park. The museums and houses along the way open to the public have varied hours. Most are open only during the warmer months (late spring to early autumn), most are closed on Sundays, Mondays, and holidays, and most charge admission. To plan your trip, write or telephone the Mayor and Council of New Castle, 220 Delaware Street, New Castle, Delaware, 19720, 302-328-4804.

ACCESS

New Castle can be reached by DE 9, 141, or 273. Once in town, drive southeast along Delaware Street to the historic area and park your car near the Court House.

The Court House, built by the British in New Castle in 1732, is the nation's oldest statehouse.

TRAIL

Begin at the old Court House, with the flags of the Netherlands, Sweden, Great Britain, and the United States flying from the front balcony. Originally built in 1732, it has been restored to its 1804 appear-

51

ance based on a drawing by Benjamin Henry Latrobe. Mason and Dixon, in their surveys of 1763–1767 in which they recalculated Penn's original land grant, used the spire atop the cupola of the Court House as the center of the twelve-mile radial circle that forms Delaware's northern boundary with Pennsylvania. That line became famous for dividing the slave states of the south from the free states of the north. (Hike number 4 in Walter S. Carpenter, Jr. State Park goes by the very point where the twelve-mile radius intersects the Mason-Dixon Line.)

In 1775, the colonial assembly, meeting in this building, appointed delegates to the Continental Congress. News of the signing of the Declaration of Independence was read from the balcony the following year. On July 4, 1776, units of the Kent County militia and the Delaware Regiment ransacked the building of all symbols of the English crown and burned them in the street. The new state assembly met here from 1776 to 1777 and drafted the first Constitution of Delaware; it is America's oldest statehouse.

The building is now under the control of the Delaware Division of Archives and Cultural Affairs and is operated as a free museum. But it is still a working building — the New Castle County Court meets here occasionally and community organizations and firms rent parts of the building. The west wing, dating from 1845, houses the Court House Shop. Stepping inside, I expected to find the usual souvenirs of postcards and miniature spoons. Instead, I discovered a notable collection of old books, maps, and prints of early Americana, children's literature, and books on natural history, regional history, travel, and a host of other subjects. Free maps of old New Castle can be obtained here, too. Margaret Baker, the proprietor, operates from a cluttered desk behind tall stacks of used books and runs her business based upon old-fashioned values. When I had gathered an armful of books I wanted, I discovered I did not have enough cash to pay for them. I asked if she accepted credit cards.

"No, but we accept checks," she said.

I replied I didn't have any checks with me.

"That's O.K.," she answered without pause. "You look like an honest man. Take the books and send me a check later."

Back outside, turn left on Delaware Street and cross Market Street to the Town Hall, built in 1823. City Council still meets in the second-story chamber. The arch and two rooms on the first floor were designed

52

as a fire station. Walk through the arch into Market Square, used as a market as early as 1682, the year William Penn arrived in town. The statue of Penn in the square shows him holding the symbolic gifts of his New World land grant — "turf and twig and water and soyl."

Turn right across Second Street to the Presbyterian Church. Built by the English in 1707, it absorbed an earlier Dutch Reformed Church that dates back to 1657. Graves of early worshipers are scattered around the foundation and about the churchyard. Unmarked, cracked tombstones in the burial ground are from the Dutch era; several marked graves are from the pre-Revolutionary period. The church and grounds are open to visitors.

Walk back across Second Street, Market Square, and cobbled Market Street to The Green or Market Plaine. Designed to serve as a common ground for the townspeople to graze their livestock, The Green became a center for "great fairs and weekly markets" in early times. The tradition continues even today; on my last visit, The Green was the scene of the Lions Club's Art-on-The-Green festival.

The long, two-story brick building on The Green, facing Market Street and Square, was built by the federal government in 1809 to serve as the U.S. Arsenal. In 1831, troops from Fort Delaware on Pea Patch Island (see the next hike) were garrisoned here temporarily after their fort was destroyed. After the Mexican War, the building served as a school and later as a restaurant.

Past the Arsenal, at the end of The Green, enter the cemetery of Immanuel Church through the gate. The graveyard contains the tomb of George Read, one of three New Castle men who signed the Declaration of Independence, and other early statesmen. The church itself, with its landmark town clock, was rebuilt in 1982 after a disastrous fire gutted the interior in 1980. When it was founded in 1689, it was the first Church of England parish in Delaware. Episcopalian today, the church is open to visitors.

Exit the graveyard through the Market Street gate, turn left, walk to the end of the block, and turn left on Harmony Street. Go to the next intersection (Third Street), cross it, and turn left on the rising-and-falling brick sidewalk. The octagonal Victorian Library (1890) houses a museum. Most of the other buildings on Third Street facing The Green date from the late eighteenth or early nineteenth century. The newest is the Rodney House (1831) at the corner of Third Street and Silsbee Alley. The oldest is the wooden-roofed Dutch House (c. 1660),

53

the only survivor of the Dutch period of New Castle and believed to be the oldest brick dwelling in the state. Today it is a museum (a fee is charged).

Turn right on Delaware Street, go to the next block, cross Fourth Street, and arrive at Amstel House (1730), a museum of the New Castle Historical Society (fee charged). Walk across Delaware Street, turn left, and go all the way to the Delaware River. At the end of the street on the right, just beyond where the sidewalk ends, stands the original ticket office of the New Castle and Frenchtown Railroad, built in 1832, with a recreated section of track. The train replaced an earlier stage line that ran to Frenchtown, Maryland, on the Elk River, an arm of the Chesapeake. New Castle was once an important rail center, serving passengers as they shuttled from boats on the Delaware and the Elk. The seventeen-mile NC & FRR was the first railroad in the state and one of the first steam-powered passenger lines in America; the first steam locomotive on the tracks, the English-built *New Castle*, rolled along at speeds of up to ten miles per hour.

A side trip (one-half-mile round-trip) through Battery Park on the right can be taken by following the paved path along the river. Traditionally, The Battery was the site of cannon emplacements of the early 1700s designed to protect the town from pirate attacks. Sweeping views can be had across the Delaware to the New Jersey shore. Benches, picnic tables, a playground, and a small, sand beach are features of the park. Walk to the far side and then return to the foot of Delaware Street, site of the town wharf in the days when New Castle was a maritime center and one of the most important ports of entry in North America. William Penn stepped ashore here in October, 1682, with a hundred Quakers on the three hundred-ton ship *Welcome*.

With your back to the river, walk up the right side of Delaware Street and turn right at the first street — The Strand. Named after a fashionable London avenue, The Strand was the bustling waterfront street of the busy port, lined with inns, taverns, ship chandler's shops, and offices. These old buildings have been converted into private homes, and, today, The Strand is shady and quiet. The third alley on the right is Packet Alley, so-called because a wharf at the end of the little street received packet boats with passengers from Boston, New York City, and Philadelphia, who transferred here to stagecoach or train and continued on to Baltimore, Washington, or southward by way of Chesapeake Bay.

Farther along, on the left, is the George Read II House (1804), a remarkably fine example of Georgian architecture. The house is open to the public (fee charged). Continue along The Strand to Harmony Street, turn left, walk to Market Street, and turn left to return to the Court House.

Pea Patch Island

*Boat excursion and hiking on
an island in the Delaware River*

Hiking distance: 2 miles
Hiking time: 1 hour plus
Maps: USGS Delaware City;
  park map

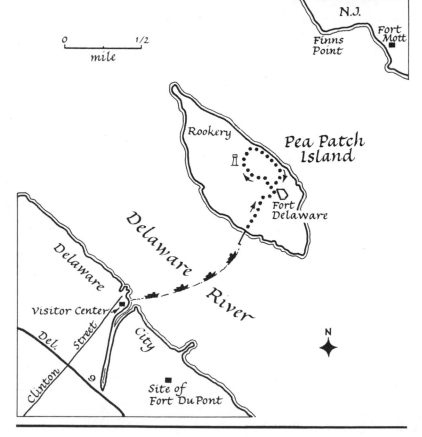

THIS SHORT WALK FEATURES AN OUTSTANDING natural area and an old fort entered on the National Registry of Historic Sites. The setting is 161-acre Pea Patch Island in the middle of the Delaware, America's widest river. The entire island is preserved as Fort Delaware State Park.

A 90-acre stand of small trees and shrubs in the northern part of Pea Patch is a specially managed natural area. The grove is separated from the rest of the island by a strip of marshland and serves as the nesting area for many wading birds. The rookery is the largest in Delaware and is believed to be one of the largest in the northeastern United States. More than seven thousand birds nest here annually. Just about every large wading bird listed for the Delaware Bason comes here to build nests and raise their young: great blue heron, little blue heron, Louisiana heron, black-crowned and yellow-crowned night herons, glossy ibis, great egret, snowy egret, and cattle egret. This area is the only known place in Delaware where black-crowned night herons nest. The island houses the largest breeding population of cattle egrets in the entire Middle Atlantic region.

Entry to the rookery itself is by permit only, for the birds are easily disturbed by human intruders. A low tower on our trail enables hikers to view the colony from across the marsh. During nesting season (generally from mid-March to mid-July), the tangled branches and heavy underbrush are alive with the long-legged waders. Be sure to bring your binoculars.

The high ground on the southern part of Pea Patch is the site of Fort Delaware, a granite bastion designed to protect the sea approaches to the upriver ports of New Castle, Wilmington, and Philadelphia. The first fortification on the island was a star-shaped fort built in 1823. It was one of a series of coastal forts placed at strategic locations in the first half of the nineteenth century to defend Atlantic seaports. Pea Patch Island, lying in the center of the broad Delaware, was considered a key to the defense of the river. Military planners linked the range of the fort's guns with sister batteries on the mainland — Fort Du Pont on the Delaware shore and Fort Mott on the New Jersey side.

Old Fort Delaware was completely destroyed by fire in 1831. The post's soldiers were transferred to the United States Arsenal in New Castle (see hike 8) while the army constructed new defenses on the island. The larger, five-sided stone fort, still standing on the site today, was built in the 1850s and was garrisoned at the outbreak of the Civil War.

Typically, institutions such as military installations, prisons, mental hospitals, and universities are sources of both income and concern for local residents. Fort Delaware was no exception. The post never came under attack during its long history, so the men stationed there often had time on their hands between their regular, often boring, soldierly duties. Elijah Brooks, editor in the early 1800s of the Salem *Messenger* across the river in New Jersey, referred to troops at the nearby garrison as "desperadoes from that den of iniquity, Fort Delaware."

The post entered its most famous (some say notorious) era during the Civil War when it served as a prison for southern sympathizers and Confederate prisoners of war. The mainland civilians' concerns reached new levels because of fear the prisoners would break loose, join northern Copperheads, and seize control of the river and its cities. Such a strategy may have made sense militarily, but the Confederates were in no shape to carry it out. Twelve thousand of them were jammed into damp cells on a marshy, mosquito-ridden island. Conditions were deplorable and disease was rampant. No more than a small handful of the prisoners were able to perform their duties at any given time. S. Weir Mitchell, a Union Army surgeon stationed at Fort Delaware,

Long vistas of the broad Delaware River and the low New Jersey shore can be enjoyed from Pea Patch Island.

wrote in his diary that "the living had more life upon them than in them." Of the many southerners who died at the fort, most were buried across the Delaware at Finns Point, New Jersey, now a national cemetery.

Around the turn of the century, Fort Delaware was modernized with large disappearing rifles mounted in concrete emplacements. The southern half of the fort was covered to accommodate these huge pieces of artillery, designed to swing down out of sight while being loaded. By World War II the entire fort, even the disappearing rifles, had become obsolete. In 1944, the post was decommissioned; it was acquired by the state of Delaware about seven years later.

ACCESS

The Delaware Division of Parks and Recreation operates a ferry to Pea Patch Island from their Fort Delaware State Park Visitor Center in Delaware City. The Visitor Center is at the foot of Clinton Street, opposite the post office. The ferry, the *Miss Kathy*, runs on weekends and holidays from the last weekend in April through the last weekend in September. Wednesday trips can also be arranged for groups. Call the park at 302-834-7941 for additional information. Round-trip fare is $2.50 for adults and $1.25 for children.

TRAIL

Because of shallow mud flats encircling the island, the *Miss Kathy* docks at the end of a long wharf. On the landward end of the wharf, a tractor with passenger trailers meets the boat to carry visitors to the front gate of Fort Delaware. Of course, you could also walk. The way leads for almost one-half mile through a brackish marsh characterized by an almost pure stand of phragmites. Towering as high as fifteen feet, this supple reed that rustles with the slightest breeze is supported by a network of underground rhizomes or rootstalks, which store nutrients and give the plant a head start each growing season. Phragmites usually turns green and begins sprouting early in the spring, before other plants begin leafing out. The creeping rhizomes can extend a stand of reeds by as much as thirty feet a year.

When you reach the moated fort, turn left, walk across the open area, and enter the woods on the Wading Bird Trail. Built by the Youth Conservation Corps, this wide footpath meanders through a bottomland hardwood forest of red maple, wild cherry, sassafras, sumac, buttonbush, and box elder. A few red cedar are also seen. The distant sound of a navigational horn on the Delaware mingles with the calls of catbirds and thrushes.

You will soon reach the wooden tower that allows you to view the heronry across the marsh. With binoculars, the large nests, often with a couple of downy young in them, are plainly visible. Adults fly about constantly or call loudly from their perches.

To continue, follow the trail as it skirts marshland and then passes a rock-strewn beach affording magnificent views across the broad river to the New Jersey shore. Binoculars will help you pick out the low profile of Fort Mott (now a state park), with Finns Point just to the north. The beach here and even this trail may be submerged during very high tides or floods.

Come out of the woods and angle right across the open space to Fort Delaware's front entrance. Take the time to tour the old fort before walking back to the wharf. The *Miss Kathy's* last departure for the mainland is at 6 p.m.

Lums Pond State Park

A circuit hike around Delaware's largest body of fresh water

Hiking distance: 6 or 7 miles, depending on side trail
Hiking time: 4-4½ hours
Maps: USGS Saint Georges; park map

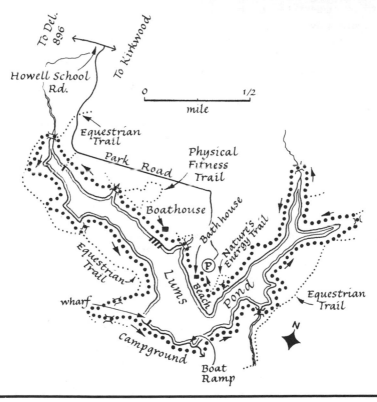

LUMS POND BEGAN AS A MAN-MADE MILLPOND IN
the early 1800s. It was enlarged and dredged in the 1820s to serve as
a feeder pond for the lock system on the nearby Chesapeake and
Delaware Canal. When the canal was changed to a sea level route, the
locks were eliminated and Lums Pond lost its usefulness to maritime
commerce. The two hundred-acre pond and the land south of it were
declared surplus property by the U.S. Army Corps of Engineers and
sold to the state of Delaware. The state park was created in the mid-
1960s and has been developed since that time as an outdoor recreation
center.

The 1,200-acre park lies in populous northern Delaware and receives
heavy use on summer weekends and holidays, but it is often overlooked
by hikers. One of my walks in the park was on Memorial Day weekend;
the beach, picnic areas, boat launching areas, and campground were
crowded with people, yet I did not encounter another hiker on the
trail. At places along the shore the only sounds you hear are the lapping
of gentle waves and the murmuring of the breeze through the trees.
Many species of mammals, birds, reptiles, amphibians, fishes, and
insects abound in the pond and adjacent fields and forests. The large
trees in the park serve as home to colonies of wild honeybees and as
nesting sites for great horned owls. All three of the mimic thrushes
found in eastern North America (northern mockingbird, gray catbird,
and brown thrasher) are common in the park. Orchard orioles, indigo
buntings, and wood thrushes can be observed in the proper habitats.
The black rat snake is the most frequently encountered terrestrial
reptile. Mammals likely to be spotted are eastern cottontails, woodchucks, and raccoons. Beavers, uncommon in Delaware, are present
but are rarely seen by park visitors.

When you walk this trail keep in mind two important considerations.
First, Lums Pond is one of the few state parks in Delaware that allows
hunting. If you must hike here during hunting season, wear bright
clothing. Second, the meadows and hedgerows along the trail provide
ideal habitats for ticks. Expect to encounter ticks at any season, even
on mild winter days, but be especially alert in spring and early summer
when scores of ticks can be picked up in certain areas. You should
check yourself carefully after you walk and remove any attached or
unattached ticks. Also, be sure to inspect your youngsters and dog.

Part of this walk traverses the park's nature trail. A descriptive
leaflet with paragraphs that correspond to numbered stations is available from park rangers. The hike I recommend begins at the swimming

beach and proceeds counterclockwise around the pond. Access to the trail, however, can be gained at several points. For example, if you camped at Lums Pond you could easily pick up the trail from the campground. However, the pleasant thing about beginning at the swimming beach is that you will end there. What better way to cap off a walk around Lums Pond than to swim in its cool waters?

ACCESS

Lums Pond State Park is 7.6 miles south of Newark near the town of Kirkwood. From Newark, take DE 896 south through Glasgow. Go 2.3 miles beyond Glasgow and turn left off of DE 896 onto Howell School Road. The entrance is on the right, 0.4 mile from the junction with DE 896. Take the park road 1.6 miles to the swimming beach parking lot.

TRAIL

To reach our trail, walk toward the pond on the broad, paved path, past the public bathhouse and snack bar. Before reaching the sand swimming beach, turn right (west) into the picnic area and angle toward the shore. You will soon find a network of pathways converging upon a wooden bridge crossing one of the many arms of Lums Pond. Cross the bridge and immediately turn left onto the gravel trail. Ignore the other paths going straight and to the right.

In one-fourth mile, you reach the park boathouse where canoes, sailboats, rowboats, and pedal boats can be rented in the summer. Turn left onto the paved path and walk to the docks. Then turn right onto the concrete sidewalk, go to the end of the dock area, and continue on the graveled path. This area is very picturesque since the trail is built close to the water's edge.

A sign on the right after one-fourth mile indicates the entrance to the fitness trail. Long popular in Europe, these specialized trails for building physical fitness are new to the United States. If you want, your walking distance can be increased one mile by taking the physical fitness trail. It returns to this point after twenty exercise stations. You can jog or walk at your own pace, stopping periodically to work out at rustic equipment along the way. Markers illustrate the exercises and explain how to participate at your level of ability.

Back on the shoreline trail, cross an arched footbridge and immediately turn left through a grassy picnic area. Ignore the gravel path that goes straight. On the far side of the picnic area, a sign indicates where the trail reenters the woods. Continue along the shore, passing a fishing wharf and crossing the trail connecting the wharf with a parking area. Beavers prowl this part of the pond; evidences of recent tree cutting can be seen near the shore.

Leave the woods and enter a small grassy area with several picnic tables. On the far side of this opening, the park's equestrian trail comes in from the right and joins the hiking trail to cross the upper reaches of the pond by a dike covered with broken asphalt. Our path turns sharply left and crosses the dike on a berm. This area is a favorite spot for fishermen and you will likely see several anglers trying for bass, bluegill, crappie, catfish, or pickeral.

When off the berm, again turn sharply left. The trail soon forks, with the bridle trail going to the right and our path continuing to hug the shore to the left. This part of the park is largely undeveloped, enabling the hiker to enjoy long stretches of solitude. Grand vistas of quiet water framed by red birch trees appear at bends in the trail. The path stays mainly near the shore and is canopied by large beech and oak trees. Occasional sections, however, cross old open fields. The fields are filled with sun-loving wild flowers during the growing season. In just a short time, you can discover hawkweeds, clovers, hop clovers, chickweeds, speedwells, wood-sorrels, asters, and goldenrods. These old fields are favorite areas for praying mantises to lay their egg cases; in late autumn and winter look for the hardened, brown, foamlike masses on stems and twigs. The eggs within the cases wait in silence for the warmer and longer spring days before hatching into young mantids.

The equestrian trail remains close to the footpath and on three occasions the two trails brush each other; but, they always return to their own orbits around the pond. In each of these instances, choose the path to the left and you will remain on the hiking trail close to the shoreline. The footpath is invariably narrower and in some places is almost choked with Japanese honeysuckle, blackberry, and other woody vines and shrubs. Some bushwhacking may be necessary.

Our trail crosses a wet meadow filled with ferns and sedges, then climbs slightly to cross an old field. After the third brush with the bridle trail, the path descends and crosses a deeply gullied stream on a wooden bridge, then enters a forest dominated by mature beech, hickory, and oak trees. The understory is strikingly open and spring wild flowers grow abundantly in the rich forest humus.

After 2½ miles, the trail turns sharply right, away from the water, to avoid an extensive marsh bordering the pond. The pathway leads out of the woods and then joins the horse trail at the beginning of the field. Turn left onto the bridle path and follow it for one-fourth mile. At one point, the two trails diverge briefly so that foot travelers can cross a stream on a bridge while riders are directed upstream to a ford. When the trails split again, the footpath leads left into the woods and the broad bridle path stays mainly straight in the field.

Our trail eventually comes upon the park's campground. Turn left immediately after crossing a bridge over a gullied stream and stay on the trail in the woods. The path going straight leads to a mowed area in the campground. The trail stays close to the water and skirts a fishing wharf. The wharf serves not only fishermen but also birders. It overlooks a former forested area that was inundated by the impoundment's rising waters. The dead snags, old tree trunks, and fallen logs provide ideal perches for birds. In the warmer months, barn swallows and tree swallows are usually skimming across the water in search of flying insects. Fishing birds such as great egrets, cattle egrets, great blue herons, and belted kingfishers are also commonly seen here. Eastern kingbirds, starlings, red-winged blackbirds, and woodpeckers (especially common flickers) are often spotted on the snags and along the shore. In addition, logs slanting out of the water usually are crowded with basking turtles, some of them quite large. Lums Pond supports a sizable turtle population; almost any visual sweep of the water's surface will reveal turtles' heads protruding above the water as they swim along.

Beyond the campground, our trail continues for one-quarter mile to a boat launching ramp. Cross at the lower end of the parking lot. The road to the right leads shortly to U.S. 301 — DE 71. After the boat launching ramp, you reenter a wild, undeveloped portion of the pond shore. The land is low and swampy here; expect muddy conditions during most of the year. Clubmosses and Christmas ferns grow densely on either side of the trail. This is an excellent place to be watchful and to catch a glimpse of some of the park's more wary birds and mammals, such as American woodcock, yellow-crowned night heron, bobwhite, and red-tailed hawk. Where the trail approaches open fields look for woodchuck dens. Woodchucks are common in this part of the park since they prefer to dig their burrows a few feet inside the forest at the edges of meadows and fields. These large rodents are often out during the daylight hours (except in winter) feeding on leaves and grasses.

As the trail angles northeasterly you cross the outlet from Lums

65

Pond. Shortly beyond the outlet the footpath climbs a small bank and joins the bridle trail for about two hundred yards as they both follow the dividing line between woods and fields. Then the two trails split again and the hiking path reenters the woods to the left.

The trail travels through small, second-growth trees, then leaves the woods to link again with the bridle path. The two trails cross a field, then go through a hedgerow to follow the edge of a cornfield for about a hundred feet. The footpath then crosses back through the hedgerow, descends slightly through a young, brushy forest, and crosses an inlet on a wooden bridge. A marsh at the margin of the pond is visible on your left as you descend to the bridge.

Beyond the bridge, climb an embankment and come out of the woods onto a rutted, dirt road. To the right, the road leads to the park's primitive camping area. Turn left (southwest). Stay on the road as it parallels the narrow eastern arm of the pond and then turns to the right (northwest) along the northern arm of the pond. Old fields dominate this part of the park, offering good opportunities to see killdeer, turkey vultures, American tree sparrows, and American crows.

Continue on the road for one-fourth mile. The road then turns sharply right and leads to the park's dog training area. Leave the road and go straight on a broad, well-maintained path for a short distance to the head of the northern arm. There turn left sharply and cross a small marsh on a wooden footbridge. Turn left onto the trail at the end of the bridge and reenter the woods.

Our path stays very close to the shore here. At the point where the northern arm enters the main body of the pond, the way turns sharply right and continues along the water. Cross a wooden bridge over a broad inlet. Soon thereafter our path joins with the Nature's Energy Trail, the park's interpretative trail. This pathway goes both right and left; turn left onto it, angling toward the shore, and immediately cross a short bridge over a rivulet.

You will shortly come upon station number 11 on the Nature's Energy Trail. Continue down the numbered stations (10, 9, 8, etc.) until you come to the trailhead and to a large play field. The bathhouse and the parking lot where you parked your car are visible ahead. Follow the edge of the field to the beach for a swim before returning to your vehicle.

Chesapeake and Delaware Canal

Along a maritime avenue, still bustling after more than 150 years

Hiking distance: 7¼ miles
Hiking time: 3½ hours
Maps: USGS Elkton and Saint
Georges

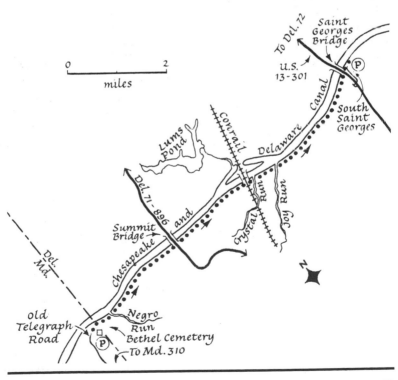

THE CHESAPEAKE AND DELAWARE CANAL, OR THE
C&D as it is called by almost everybody, is a remarkable structure
that serves a multitude of purposes. First and foremost, it is a working
waterway, wide and deep enough to handle large, ocean-going ships.
Owned and operated by the U.S. Army Corps of Engineers, it is a
crucial link in the coastwise shipping commerce of the United States.
The canal shaves almost three hundred miles off the water journey
between Philadelphia and Baltimore and eliminates the ocean route
around Cape Henlopen and Cape Charles. The passage of freighters,
barges, tugs, naval ships, fishing boats, motorboats, sailboats, and
yachts combined makes the C&D one of the busiest canals in the
world. Over 22,000 vessels sail through in an average year, including
many of foreign registry.

The canal also vitally affects the surrounding land and its people.
Although the influence is not as great today, in bygone days, the towns
and communities along the water owed their existence to the canal.
Showboats and floating stores visited the wharves. Canal men and
their families comprised most of the townspeople. Inwardly narrow
in outlook yet lying next to a great avenue of world commerce, the
communities contained both provincial and cosmopolitan elements. A
sense of this past can be obtained by strolling the streets of Chesapeake
City, Maryland — the headquarters of canal pilots — or of Delaware
City, Delaware, where the only remaining canal lock can still be seen.

Slashing across the peninsula and creating, in effect, a large island
of the southern portion of the land, the C&D has become a natural
and cultural boundary between upper and lower Delmarva. (In keeping
with this tradition, it is used as such in this book.) The southern
portion is set apart from the mainland to the north, like another country.
The region is tied to the worlds of water and of farmland and to the
unique ways and values that link engenders. Towns are small, population densities are low, and there are no interstate highways. Northern
Delawareans jokingly call the southern part of their state "slower Delaware." The northern portion offers many special, if somewhat different, features and seems more oriented to the modern, faster-paced
world of the late twentieth century. There are few farms, resulting in
an influx of urban ways and modes. Lying athwart the great northeastern megalopolis, the region is crisscrossed by interstates and commercial strips. Some say even the weather changes when you cross the canal.

Augustine Herman (or Herrman or Heermans) was the first to envi-
sion a canal linking the Chesapeake Bay and the Delaware River, and

he published such a proposal in 1661. He was in a unique position to assess all the possible routes this canal might take. Born in what is now Czechoslovakia, a mapmaker and surveyor by trade, he was serving as the Dutch envoy from new Amsterdam to the English colony of Maryland when Lord Baltimore, proprietor of Maryland, commissioned him to make a map of the area. Herman labored for ten years in the trackless wilderness, mapping not only Maryland but also what is today Delaware and much of Virginia. Lord Baltimore was so pleased with the map when it was published in 1670 that he called it "the best mapp that was ever Drawn of any Country Whatsoever," and he granted Herman 13,000 acres of land along a broad river in northeastern Maryland. Herman named the river after his fatherland, Bohemia, and called his home Bohemia Manor. From his estate he pursued his dreams of uniting the two great bodies of water — the Chesapeake Bay and the Delaware River.

First, he laid out a cart road connecting his Maryland grant with Appoquinimink Creek and the town of New Castle on the Delaware River. Known as the River Road or the Old Man's Road, this route was one of the earliest links between the Delaware River and the Chesapeake Bay. His canal plans, however, were never realized.

The idea of a canal resurfaced in 1788, when a youthful United States was eager to accomplish grand works and to demonstrate national achievements. The Chesapeake and Delaware Canal Company was founded in Philadelphia, and construction began in 1804. The work halted two years later because of lack of funds. The ditch lay unfinished for seventeen years until construction resumed; the canal finally opened to traffic on October 17, 1829.

Competition came swiftly three years later when the New Castle and Frenchtown Railroad began servicing roughly the same route. Unlike most other parts of the country where railroads won the economic battle for passenger and freight revenue however, the C&D Canal Company survived and the NC&FRR failed.

The federal government purchased the canal in 1919 to modernize and enlarge it for stream-powered ships. The U.S. Army Corps of Engineers were given control of the waterway. Their first tasks were to eliminate the locks and to deepen and widen the channel. Removing the locks eliminated the need for feeder ponds, such as Lums Pond (see the previous hike), along the length of the canal. Today, the C&D is 450 feet wide, 35 feet deep, and almost 14 miles long. The east end enters the Delaware River at Reedy Point, and the west end empties into Back Creek at Chesapeake City, thence into the Elk River and the Chesapeake Bay.

Both banks of the canal are lined with a number of unpaved service roads. The roads near the water are passable by cars and are used by fishermen and other pleasure seekers. The roads farther up the banks are generally rougher and less frequently traveled. Side roads connect all these routes at intervals. This hike follows the service roads along the south bank, beginning in Maryland but soon entering Delaware. Other walks are possible along the north bank and along other sections of the south bank.

Land bordering the C&D in both states is part of a public hunting area. Care should be exercised during hunting season. There are no trees of any appreciable size along the canal; walking here on sunny summer days can be hot and thirst provoking. Guard against sunburn and carry a canteen of water. This hike is best done with two cars to avoid retracing your route.

ACCESS

From Elkton, drive east on U.S. 40, entering Delaware and turning right (south) on DE 72 after 6.0 miles. Go 3.8 miles and turn right (south) on U.S. 13 and 301. Cross the C&D Canal on the high-level Saint Georges Bridge. On the south side, turn right at the first opportunity onto Road 34C into the hamlet of South Saint Georges (2.2 miles from where you first picked up U.S. 13 and 301). Road 34C circles under the bridge and, after 0.3 mile, comes to Road 34B; turn left. Follow Road 34B 0.4 mile to where it ends overlooking the C&D. Turn right onto a paved street and drive close to where it intersects with the dirt service road along the canal. Park the first car along the shoulder of the paved street.

If coming from Newark, drive south on DE 72 for 9.1 miles to U.S. 13 and 301. Turn right (south) and follow the above directions.

To reach the trail head, drive the second car back to U.S. 13 and 301 and turn right (south). After 3.0 miles, the highways split; keep right on U.S. 301 and DE 896. In 3.5 miles, you will come upon a major intersection in the little village of Mount Pleasant. U.S. 301 goes to the left and DE 896 turns right; DE 71 goes both left and right. Continue straight (west) onto Road 432, leaving the federal and state highways behind. Go through a crossroads and enter Maryland after 3.6 miles; the road becomes MD 310. Drive for only 0.1 mile

70

and then turn right onto Old Telegraph Road. Follow this road for 2.7 miles, pass a crossroads, and arrive at Bethel Cemetery on the right just before dead-ending at the canal. Park your car along the entrance drive to the cemetery, being careful not to block access.

TRAIL

Walk the short distance along Old Telegraph Road toward the canal. A cross-shaped stone monument on the right overlooks the C&D and commemorates the Bethel Methodist Church. The 1849 church house was torn down in 1965 in order to widen the waterway. Turn right (east) on the dirt service road and descend to the water level. Later, side roads will allow you to either stay near the canal or to walk along one of the upper service roads. The first side road is slightly more than one-half mile from the trail head, near where Negro Run enters the canal. Short, wooden wharves jutting into the canal here and elsewhere help fishermen capture crappie, perch, catfish, drum, and largemouth bass. In the spring, barn swallows build their nests on the beams under the wharves. They usually can be seen zipping across the water in pursuit of insects. Other common birds along the canal include great blue herons, black-crowned night herons, fish crows, eastern kingbirds, rock doves, and bobwhites.

You will enter Delaware in about one-fourth mile and will pass under the Summit Bridge after about another two miles. Constructed in 1960, this bridge carries DE 71 and 896 over the canal on a four-lane, high-level crossing; the span between the piers is 560 feet. As its name implies, Summit Bridge is near the subdivide separating the Chesapeake and Delaware watersheds. For about the next 1½ miles, the C&D passes through the Deep Cut; the bluff on the north bank is approximately sixty feet high and is an excellent place for fossil hunting. Most of the fossils are marine animals or their remains (such as shark's teeth, clams, snails, and mud-shrimps) dating from the Cretaceous age (65-135 million years ago).

Beyond the Deep Cut, walk under the Conrail Railroad Bridge, one of the longest railway lift bridges in the world. With a horizontal clearance of 548 feet, the span took four years to build. It opened in 1966. Just east of the bridge, a culvert carries Crystal Run under the path. About one-half mile farther, Joy Run flows into the canal.

The houses of South Saint Georges crowd the bank as you approach

71

the Saint Georges Bridge. This bridge is the oldest (1942) and most attractive of those across the canal. Continue for about another one-quarter mile to the paved road on the right where you parked the other car.

Chesapeake Bay

Redden State Forest

Eastern Neck Island

A walk through an island refuge to an isolated shore on the Chester River

Hiking distance: 1 mile
Hiking time: ¾ hour
Maps: USGS Langford Creek; refuge map

To Rock Hall

Md. 445

Eastern Neck

Neck Narrows

Chester

Eastern

Tubby Cove

0   1/2
         mile

Chesapeake

N

Bogle Cove

Bogles Wharf Rd.

River

P

Refuge Headquarters

Bay

Eastern Neck Island

EASTERN NECK ISLAND ILLUSTRATES THE CONTIguity and contrast between the natural and the overcivilized world. If you stand at the edge of the Chesapeake Bay on the island's northwestern shore on a clear day the industrial smokestacks that ring Baltimore are visible across the water. Eastern Neck's immediate neighbor across the Chester River to the southwest, Kent Island, anchors the eastern end of the Chesapeake Bay Bridge. Because of this connection to major population centers, Kent wrestles with the stresses of traffic congestion, noise pollution, and land and waterfront development.

By contrast, Eastern Neck Island, with a history of human habitation stretching back at least 2,700 years, remains a wild land where the patterns of nature assert themselves with striking clarity. It is a haven for indigenous and migrating wildlife. The island's tranquil bays and coves, tidal flats, open fields, woodlands, and great expanses of marshlands support a remarkable diversity and abundance of life.

The island's forests are one of the few remaining isolated habitats for Delmarva fox squirrels. These large squirrels, a subspecies of the eastern fox squirrel, are found only on the Delmarva Peninsula and are listed as an endangered species by the federal government. Endangered birds found on the island, at least occasionally, are bald eagles and ospreys. I have seen nesting ospreys in the vicinity of Tubby Cove.

Perhaps the most spectacular wildlife scene enjoyed by most visitors, and the one for which Eastern Neck is noted, includes the thousands of whistling swans that winter on the island each year. The concentrations of stately swans are but a part of the large numbers of waterfowl that use the area. Canada goose, mute swan, bufflehead, widgeon, pintail, mallard, black duck, canvasback, greater scaup, ruddy duck, oldsquaw, and white-winged scoter can be seen between October and March. Waterfowl populations usually peak in November.

The preservation of the 2,285-acre island was assured in 1962 when the area was set aside as the Eastern Neck National Wildlife Refuge. As part of the wildlife management program, only certain areas of the island are open to visitors. The area through which this hike passes is usually open but may be closed some days during the public whitetailed deer hunt. Generally, the hunt does not interfere with hikers because it is scheduled for only eight or ten scattered weekdays from October to December, but telephone the refuge office at 301-639-7056 prior to your hike during hunting season. Refuge personnel can also provide you with maps, bird lists, and information on other trails.

The headquarters building is located beyond the turn-off for the hike and is marked by signs. If the office is closed, limited brochures are usually available at the trailhead to the Trail of Life, the refuge's interpretative trail located on the left of the main refuge road just beyond Bogles Wharf Road.

If possible, hike this trail during the cooler months. Not only will you likely be rewarded by some memorable waterfowl sightings, but you will also avoid the numerous mosquitoes, deer flies, no-see-ums, and ticks. On Eastern Neck, these biting arthropods can turn any hike into a gauntlet. If you visit the island in the warmer seasons, wear repellent.

ACCESS

Eastern Neck Island lies in the upper Chesapeake at the mouth of the Chester River. It is connected to the mainland by bridge. To reach the island, drive south from Chestertown on MD 20 for 12.9 miles to the ship-building community of Rock Hall. There, turn left (south) on MD 445 for the drive down Eastern Neck. After 5.7 miles you will approach the bridge across Eastern Neck Narrows. Continue straight for another 1.1 miles, then turn left onto Bogles Wharf Road. After 0.1 mile, park your car in the gravel lot on the right.

TRAIL

The trail begins across the road (opposite the parking lot) and meanders through the woods in a northeasterly direction. Initially the way is heavily shaded by pines, sweetgum, and dogwood. Eventually, you enter a field where the path goes through tall grasses.

Marshland or open water is occasionally visible on either side of the trail. After one-half mile, you enter another wooded area and then arrive at a small beach along the Chester River. The beach is mainly made of old oyster shells with interspersed seams of sand and pebbles. It is a lovely, secluded shore, a place where, as Thoreau wrote, you "shall hear only the wind whispering among the reeds."

Your first impression undoubtedly will be of the river — here, a great two-mile wide tidal arm of the bay. The Chester is the last free-flowing river to enter the Chesapeake. It has escaped damming and channelization, and its bottomland, bordering swamps, and non-tidal wetlands have not been ditched and drained. Some boats may be on the water and you will be able to see a few minor evidences of civilization, such as fields and dwellings, on the opposite shore; but, by and large, your view is of a pristine landscape little changed in thousands of years. Take time to explore the beach and surroundings. The longer you stay, the more you will discover. A short walk to the left leads to an inlet surrounded by a broad marsh. Walking right brings you to a point that affords a sweeping view of Bogle Cove, one of the myriad indented hideaways lining the Chester.

After you feel sufficiently braced by the fresh air and stirring beauty of these shores, turn and retrace your way.

Overcup Oak Nature Trail

An interpretative trail to a majestic tree in Tuckahoe State Park

Hiking distance: ¾ mile
Hiking time: ¾ hour
Maps: USGS Ridgely; park map

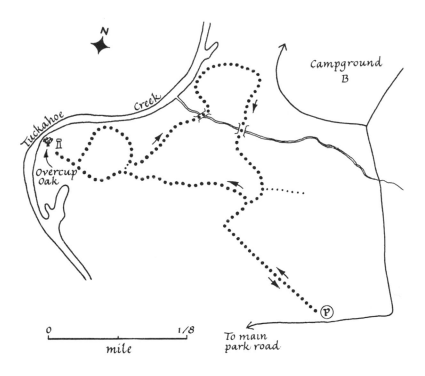

THIS SHORT TRAIL BRINGS YOU TO A GRAND OVER-
cup oak, a venerable monarch that has lived by the side of Tuckahoe
Creek for over 2¼ centuries. Overcup oaks are seldom seen by hikers.
They normally grow only in lowland habitats such as sloughs, river
swamps, floodplains, bayous, and other bottoms — areas where foot
travel is difficult if not impossible. The species has a wide range,
occurring from New Jersey south through the Coastal Plain to Texas
and north up the Mississippi Valley to southern Illinois and Indiana,
but, because it grows only in heavy, poorly drained soils, its distribution
is sporadic. A 1972 study of Maryland trees listed the overcup oak as
"rare" for the state.

The story of the Tuckahoe oak is marked by confusion and can be
surmised only by conjecture. The tree perhaps began to grow in the
deep shade of a primal forest under giant trees reaching upwards to
two hundred feet. It alone survived and today is surrounded by much
smaller trees; it is clearly the largest living thing in the area. Why
loggers spared this oak is unknown. When the great trees that were
its neighbors had been cut down, it likely grew more quickly in the
bright sunlight and developed an impressive crown stretching outwards
118 feet, typical of oak found in the open.

For years it was misidentified as the closely related swamp white
oak. Only recently was it correctly determined to be an overcup oak
— distinguished by narrow leaves with rounded lobes and by the
distinctive acorn almost completely covered by the cup. It reigned for
a time as the largest overcup oak in the nation as recognized by the
American Forestry Association. In 1984 another, slightly larger speci-
men in South Carolina was declared superior. Signs and other printed
material still refer to the Maryland tree as the national champion
however.

The dethronement does not detract from the majesty of this tree
along the Tuckahoe. Soaring almost twelve stories high, with a circum-
ference of over 22½ feet and a diameter of over 7 feet, it is awesomely
impressive. No one is really sure how long overcup oaks can live; other
oaks are known to be five hundred to one thousand years old or more
and show no decline. If the same yardstick is applied, then this noble
tree, which appears healthy and vigorous, is just entering its prime.
The managers of the Tuckahoe State Park, responsible for the care of
the tree, are doing all they can for its well-being. Hikers are advised
against approaching too close because foot traffic can compact the wet,
bottomland soil, creating potential erosional problems and upsetting

the ability of the tree's roots to take in water and nutrients. Cables intertwine throughout the tree's enormous crown, helping prevent the heavy, ancient limbs from snapping during high winds. A lightning rod has been installed along the back side of the trunk.

The path leading to the oak is an interpretative trail that winds through both upland and bottomland forest. It is an excellent walk for families with young children. Numbered stations along the way are described in a pamphlet. The posts are placed to tell the story of many of the park's trees — their names, characteristics, commercial uses, etc. The trail and accompanying guide were laid out in 1981 by Eric Moore Belknap as an Eagle Scout project. A box at the trailhead designed to dispense the pamphlets had been vandalized at the time of my last visit; they can also be obtained from rangers or at the park office.

ACCESS

From Denton, drive west on MD 404 for 6.0 miles. Turn right (east) on MD 480, go just 0.1 mile, then turn left on Eveland Road. After 3.1 miles, come to a "T" intersection with Crouse Mill Road; turn right, then left again immediately onto Cherry Lane. Continue for 0.8 mile, then turn left into the park road that leads to the picnic area and the campground. After 0.2 mile, turn right at the first intersection and drive another 0.2 mile. Park your car in a small, grassy lot on the left, opposite the sign that says "National Champion Overcup Oak."

If coming from Centreville, drive east on MD 304 for 6.5 miles to the hamlet of Ruthsburg. There turn right (south) on MD 481. After 2.0 miles, enter Tuckahoe State Park by turning left onto Crouse Mill Road. The road forks after crossing Blackston Branch on a wooden bridge downstream from Tuckahoe Lake. Keep left (on Crouse Mill Road), cross Tuckahoe Creek on another wooden bridge, and turn left onto Cherry Lane (1.7 miles from MD 481). Follow the above directions to the trailhead parking lot.

TRAIL

Follow the path across the field, turn right through a hedgerow at the edge of the woods, and walk along the margin of the field. Green arrows mounted on posts point the way. Just beyond station 3 you will turn sharply left into the forest; the path ahead will bring you back to this spot later.

81

The trail descends slightly into a lowland and veers left beyond station 7. The path going straight would bring you in a few steps to the return loop. The nature trail is covered with bark mulch and bordered by logs here to keep hikers out of the mud.

After passing through a grove of tall pawpaw, the trail turns right, and a side spur leads straight to an observation platform near the mighty overcup oak growing in a swampy bend of Tuckahoe Creek. The tree bursts forth with tiny flowers in March or April, and the acorns mature by September or October. As with other species of oaks, large crops of acorns are produced only every three or four years with intervening years of limited seed production. To continue, retrace your steps to the main trail and turn left.

The main channel of Tuckahoe Creek next comes into view. At station 12, our path turns left, passing the very short side trail encountered earlier. After crossing a small branch on a long wooden bridge, the trail again follows the bank of the Tuckahoe for a short distance. The path leaves the creek and meanders to a second crossing of the small branch, this time upstream.

The nature trail comes out of the woods beyond station 20 and turns left to go to the playground and campground B. Turn right here, along the edge of the field, and approach the beginning of the trail in the vicinity of station 3. From here, it is a short walk back to the parking lot.

Martinak
State Park

*A loop through land rich in
Indian lore, featuring two spurs
to overlooks of Watts Creek and
the Choptank River*

Hiking distance: 2 miles
Hiking time: 1 hour
Map: USGS Hobbs

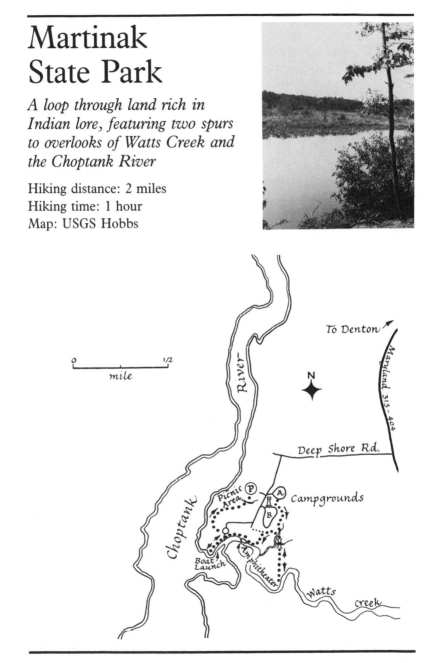

FEW OF THE WORLD'S COASTLINES ARE AS CONVO-
luted and complex as the Chesapeake shore. The land was drowned
by rising ocean waters at the end of the last Ice Age, and today's result,
especially on the Eastern Shore, is a fantastic assemblage of creeks,
rivers, bays, coves, sounds, straits, and islands. The Delmarva Peninsula is about 200 miles long, and yet within this small span there are
at least twenty-one rivers flowing into the bay. They are generally
short, arising sluggishly in upland swamps and soon broadening into
expansive tidal estuaries. The greatest of these rivers is the Choptank.

Martinak State Park lies along the upper reaches of the Choptank;
it is the only public land along the entire river. As such, it is very
popular with fishermen, who go after the catfish and bluegill, and
with boaters, who use it as a jumping-off point. Campers and picnickers
also enjoy the park. There are no designated hiking trails, but Martinak
still offers a pleasant setting for a short walk.

The trail featured here follows informal paths connecting the developed portions of the park — the campground, picnic area, boat
ramp, and amphitheater. It is impossible to get lost for long in this
small, 108-acre park, but some of the trails become confusing when
passing through these areas. Read the directions carefully. Mosquitoes
are abundant in the woods in the summer. Dogs are not permitted in
any part of Martinak.

Along the way, look for partridgeberry, moccasin-flower, Venus'
looking-glass, and other wild flowers. In the forest, wild grapes climb
toward the sunlight while big, tall pines dominate the canopy. The
deep woods provide protection for many small mammals and birds,
including whippoorwills and at least three species of owl. It is one of
the best places I know to see fish crows.

The area now parkland may have been the site of an Indian village
in olden days. Many projectile points, sherds, and other artifacts are
commonly found in the vicinity. In historic times, a Choptank Indian
reservation was downriver, where Secretary Creek enters. A major
Indian trail also was known to have passed nearby or maybe through
this area, carrying hunters, traders, and warriors between the upper
Choptank and the Delaware River near the present-day Chesapeake
and Delaware Canal.

Clearly the Choptank River has been a focal point in the landscape
of the Eastern Shore for human inhabitants since ancient times. Tiny
bands of Indians were at home on the river's banks where they established a culture based upon farming, gathering, hunting, and fishing.

84

They felled trees to create clearings where they grew crops of corn, squash, pumpkins, beans, and tobacco. The tree trunks were laboriously hollowed out to make canoes for netting and spearing fish and for capturing crustaceans and molluscs. Men of the tribe hunted in the vast wilderness for large and small game. Women and children gathered bird eggs, acorns, nuts, berries, fruits, and many different kinds of wild plants, not only for food but also for clothing, medicine, teas, and dyes. A husbandman, hunter, fisherman, gatherer, even a physician — the Indian fitted himself precisely into the patterns of the land. They knew the rivers, marshes, and forests as no other people since.

The peaceful tribe along the river was probably seminomadic, roving over rather large areas to hunt, fish, and trade. Other, more powerful tribes to the north (the Susquehannocks and the Senecas) sometimes drove them out during raids and invasions. Yet the river remained central to their tribal culture; they molded their mind, will, and spirit to the river, and they always returned to it. The river likely represented a sparkling symbol of nature's power and permanence, serving not only as a source of food and as an avenue of transportation but also, perhaps as importantly, serving as a means of inspiration, renewal, honest counsel, and solace.

Europeans met the small tribe in the early 1600s. They learned that the natives called the wide river *Choptank*, which probably means "it flows in the opposite direction" — an apt description of the long tides that surge back and forth in the channel. The people had no name for themselves; the river and its surroundings were by and large their whole context. The Europeans called them Choptanks. Much later, ethnologists and anthropologists would classify them as a subdivision of the Nanticoke and as belonging to the Algonquian linguistic family.

Relations between the Choptanks and the English were mostly cordial. The natives adopted the metal tools, weapons, and other items offered by the whites in exchange for land. The English established a comfortable economy based largely upon growing tobacco. As the colony prospered, more settlers were attracted to the region. More land was needed, said the whites, to grow tobacco and other crops. Conflicts between the races inevitably developed. The English conceived of the land in terms of ownership and use, a way of thinking alien to the Indian.

The Choptanks were soon outnumbered and outmaneuvered. Some unscrupulous whites stole land from them by guile or trickery; other

85

deals were struck after Indians were drugged with rum and whiskey. In the late 1600s, the tribe petitioned the Maryland Assembly for the land legally assigned by grants from Lord Baltimore to be set aside for them. The Choptank Reservation was created in 1698 near the present-day park. Backed into an area of only three square miles along a river they once ruled, the Choptanks still found no peace. An Indian delegation complained to the governor in 1759 that they were suffering from a shortage of food and were being violently removed from their land.

Without a strong leader and disorganized as a people, the Choptanks wandered, bewildered, mired and helpless in fear, displaced from the center of their natural world. Some became assimilated into the white or black communities developing in their old empire. Others fell prey to white Indian hunters; when other, upriver Nanticokes took up arms against the white colonists over land disputes, a general war was declared on all Indians. The peace-loving Choptanks, who had no history of warfare, were caught in the middle as whites sought vengeance and retribution. A few Indians moved deeper into the marshes, huddling in isolated and remote places where they could hide from the whites; living apart from the tribe, they gradually took on the outward signs of white society. Most started a long migration to the north, joining the Iroquois in New York and Canada and becoming incorporated into that tribe. Census figures dramatically chart the disappearance of the Choptank as a people. In 1600, an estimated 1,600 Nanticokes (including Choptanks) lived on the Eastern Shore. By 1722, only about 500 remained. Seventy years later their number had dwindled to 30.

The immense river still glides on, bearing its original Indian name, thoughtless that a way of life has vanished from the earth. On the river the silence is acute. To a visitor knowing the past, the Choptank is a vital, intimate link between himself and the ancient ones who dwelled here. With extinct rituals and unknown words, a race now vanished here enacted their own fundamental drama of life and death.

ACCESS

Martinak State Park is near Denton and can be reached by driving southeast on MD 313 and 404 for 1.9 miles. Turn right onto Deep Shore Road and then left into the park after 0.6 mile. Another 0.2 mile brings you to the entrance of picnic area A on the right. Follow the short drive to the parking lot and leave your car.

TRAIL

Walk back along the drive upon which you entered the parking lot, jog left across the park road, and enter the road leading to camping loop A. On your right is a tall water tower, the railing near the top offering a favorite lookout for crows and fish crows. Where the road forks, keep right, and turn right off the road near campsite 3 or 4. At the rear of the campsites, veer left (southeast) and, with your back to the water tower, pick up our trail as it enters the woods. A physical fitness trail in this vicinity is planned by park management.

You very soon encounter shallow ditches dug to drain water from the woodland and thereby to decrease the mosquito population. Culverts carry water under the trail in two interconnecting ditches you will cross in quick succession. More campsites are soon seen on the right as our broad path weaves between the two campground loops (A on the left and B on the right).

When you come upon a third ditch passing under the trail by means of a culvert, turn right and walk along the ditch. Step across a small side ditch and then veer left, staying behind the campsites of camping loop B on a wide trail. Descend and cross a small branch, leaving the campground behind for now.

As you approach a second branch bridged by wooden planks, the main trail turns sharply right. The spur trail straight ahead descends and eventually dead-ends at Watts Creek. Follow it south for about one-quarter mile to a quiet overlook onto a broad, winding tidal creek lined with arrowhead and rimmed by trees. The spur follows the boundary of the park (on the right) and Camp Mardela, a Church of the Brethren facility (on the left). Buildings of the church camp can be seen through the trees.

Upon returning to the main trail, turn left, descend steeply, cross the small stream as best you can, and then climb to more campsites along loop B, emerging near the rear of campsite 12. Turn left, staying behind the sites, and come across a woods road in the vicinity of campsite 9. Turn left. Where the road swerves right, continue straight on a narrow path that runs along a bluff overlooking a marsh on the left. Shortly, the trail widens and emerges at an amphitheater out over Watts Creek.

Walk straight ahead, keeping the creek on your left. Sunny areas along the bank are crowded with common mullein, its fuzzy, light green leaves ascending a tall, clublike stalk topped by yellow flowers throughout the summer. The path soon comes out into the boat launching area where there are restrooms and park benches. A second spur leads left beyond the boat ramp, following the maintenance road along the quay. At the end, a small, low, wooded headland offers splendid views of the Choptank River where Watts Creek flows into it. Oaks, holly, and cedar stand watch over the spacious river, still navigable here by large boats although we are miles from the Chesapeake.

Walk back to the boat launching area and turn left off the loop road (before reaching the large parking lot) onto a wide trail through the trees. The way soon leads to picnic area B. Walk through the picnic area and descend slightly on the far side to cross a small creek on earthen fill. This path leads directly to picnic area A where you parked your car.

Idylwild Wildlife Management Area

A scenic walk through upland fields and forests

Hiking distance: 6 miles
Hiking time: 3 hours
Maps: USGS Federalsburg and
   Seaford West

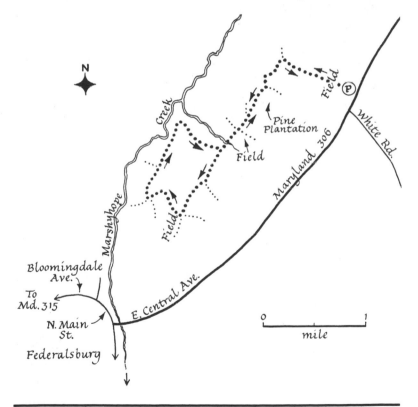

ABOUT TWENTY-FOUR MILES OF EXCELLENT WALK-
ing trails meander through the three thousand-acre Idylwild Wildlife
Management Area. Hikers, equestrians, bird watchers, wild flower
enthusiasts, and sportsmen use the area, and canoeists paddle down
Marshyhope Creek on the western boundary in spring at high water.
Visitor usage, however, is slight (except during hunting season); Idylwild is a good place to walk if you are seeking quietness and solitude.

The hike described here covers just a portion of the trails available.
It enters the area on a long spur, loops clockwise around the interior,
and then returns the same way. Because the hike lies entirely within
a public hunting area, I recommend you plan your visit at a time other
than hunting season, or on Sundays when hunting is not allowed.

ACCESS

From Denton, drive south on MD 313 for 14.6 miles to MD 315 in
the vicinity of Federalsburg. Turn left (south) on MD 315, which
becomes Bloomingdale Avenue in 0.1 mile at the Federalsburg city
limits. Continue on Bloomingdale Avenue, which curves to the right
after 0.6 mile and becomes North Main Street. Stay on North Main
Street for another 0.4 mile to the traffic signal in the center of town,
and there turn left (east) on East Central Avenue. You will leave
Federalsburg after 0.3 mile, and there the road becomes MD 306.
Continue east, passing White Road on the right after 2.6 miles and,
0.2 mile farther, turning left into the Idylwild Wildlife Management
Area parking lot.

TRAIL

Follow the path that begins at the rear of the parking lot. The trail
cuts straight across fields before entering the forest, and continues
straight until it intersects a cross trail after three-fourths mile. The
path to the right is well cleared while the path to the left is narrower
and is blocked by a steel cable drawn between poles. Turn left, walk
around the cable and hike about one-third mile.

You will come out of a small brushy area onto a broad trail going
both left and right. A plantation of young pines is directly in front.
Turn right, but take a moment to look around and memorize this trail
junction. You will be returning by the same route, and the path to the
left is not very obvious.

As you leave the pine plantation behind, our trail comes across

90

another cable barrier and enters a more mature forest dominated by oaks with a beautiful understory of tall American holly. Beyond this, a large field opens up on the left. This agricultural land is one of five such parcels on Idylwild and is custom-farmed under lease to provide more diverse habitat for wildlife.

Openings in the forest at Idylwild Wildlife Management Area provide additional food and cover for many birds and other animals.

Continue following the path at the edge of the field and the forest. Pass a side trail angling in from the right out of the woods and a cross trail near the middle of the field. Reenter the forest, and cross a little creek that flows through a culvert under the trail. At the top of the small rise beyond the creek, a major trail enters from the right. This trail is your return loop. Continue straight for now, skirting a plantation of adolescent pines on the left and an older, mostly deciduous forest on the right.

The pine plantation is soon left behind and the trail becomes shaded almost exclusively by hardwoods. An ill-defined trail comes in from the left.

About 2½ miles from the parking area, you will come upon a cross trail with an open field (a game food plot) on the far right corner. Down a trail to the left you can see a cable barricade. Turn right (west) here, keeping the field on your left, and soon becoming surrounded once more by trees. Cross two separate wetlands where the trail has been built up to escape water. These low areas support exceptional specimens of American holly. After about one-half mile, you will come upon a major cross trail. Turn right (north). Continue straight, passing a side trail to the left. The trail turns sharply to the right (east) after about three-fourths mile and comes upon a "T" junction with the return trail in about another one-half mile. Turn left and walk back to the parking lot.

Seth Demonstration Forest

An easy woodland walk featuring tall trees and wild flowers

Hiking distance: 1½ miles
Hiking time: 1 hour
Maps: USGS Easton and Trappe

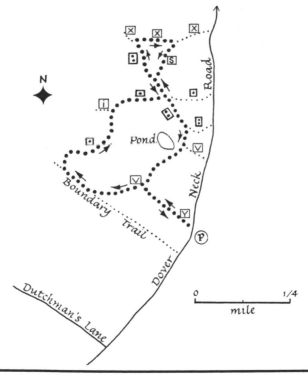

OFF THE BEATEN TRACK AND SELDOM VISITED, Seth Demonstration Forest is a charming tract of state-owned woodland in Talbot County, Maryland. Although small, Seth is a reserve for well over thirty species of trees, including many fine examples of white oak, Maryland's state tree. Surrounded almost entirely by extensive farmland, the forest also provides shelter for a variety of animals including raccoon, red and gray fox, white-tailed deer, squirrels, and owls. In the winter, nearby fields are often filled with great flocks of countless Canada geese and whistling swans feeding on the leftovers from the autumn harvest.

The demonstration forest had its beginning in 1928 when Mary W. Seth deeded 65 acres of woodland to the state. Over the years, land purchases raised the total acreage to about 124. The forest is devoted to research and education and serves as a demonstration area for modern forestry practices.

Several marked and maintained trails, laid out in the 1950s, weave through the forest. Spring is an ideal time for a walk through these woods; the spectacular wild flowers make up for the often wet conditions encountered along the trails in this season. Autumn and winter are also pleasant, but the summer mosquito populations can be overwhelming. Be sure to pack repellent.

ACCESS

At the junction with U.S. 50 in Easton, drive east on MD 331 for 0.6 mile to Chilcutt Road on the right. Turn onto Chilcutt Road, following the signs to the Easton Sanitary Landfill. After 1.4 miles, you will come upon a "T" junction with Dover Neck Road. Turn right (south), passing the entrance to the landfill on the left after 0.6 mile. Just 0.2 mile farther, Seth Demonstration Forest is on the right. No signs announce the forest, but prominent, horizontal yellow blazes are painted on trees along the boundary. Drive for another 0.5 mile and park your car on the left shoulder at the wide entrance to Rich Bottom Farm. Parking is limited, with room for only one or perhaps two vehicles. Be sure not to block entrance to the farm lane or to the mailbox. (If, while driving south on Dover Neck Road, you see a side road on the right with an electric substation on the left, you have gone beyond the forest.)

TRAIL

Cross Dover Neck Road, walk north a few feet, and enter Seth Demonstration Forest on the "Y" trail, so-called because of yellow paint blazes in the shape of a "Y" placed on trees. The trail entrance is wide and is blocked against vehicular access by a felled tree.

Walk through a mixed evergreen-deciduous forest for one-eighth mile until you come upon a "T" junction. Turn left on this new trail, marked by a yellow "V" on trees. After about another one-eighth mile, the trail ends at the edge of state land, marked by a wide, cleared swath through the woods. Here, as along the road, the forest boundary is marked by horizontal yellow blazes painted on trees. Turn right along the boundary trail.

In a short distance turn right again on a trail blazed with a single, solid yellow circle. After about one-fourth mile, our trail curves to the right as the "i" trail goes off to the left. Continue for about another one-eighth mile until you come upon a cross trail marked with two solid yellow circles, placed one above the other. Turn left.

After a short distance, the trail forks, with the "S" trail on the right. You will return to this point later by the "S" trail but for now keep left, following the double circle blaze. Our trail dead-ends at the "X" trail in less than one-eighth mile. Turn right.

Be alert for a side trail, blazed with a yellow "S," that goes off to the right just a short distance from where you turned onto the "X" trail. Turn right on the "S" trail, walk about one-eighth mile, and rejoin the double circle trail. Turn left and follow this trail past its juncture with the single circle trail. Shortly beyond, turn right on the "V" trail where the double circle trail curves to the left. A small, woodland pond can be seen in a shallow depression off to the right. The pond is likely the remains of an old borrow pit and is a favored breeding place for mosquitoes.

A side trail, also labeled "V," soon goes off to the left to exit at Dover Neck Road. Keep straight, passing a giant white oak on the right near the path. After almost one-fourth mile, you will come upon the "Y" trail on the left. Follow it back to the road and your car.

Redden
State Forest

*Level walking in Coastal
Plain forest lands*

Hiking distance: 4¾ miles
Hiking time: 2½ hours
Map: USGS Georgetown

WALKERS AND
LODGE GUESTS
——ONLY——

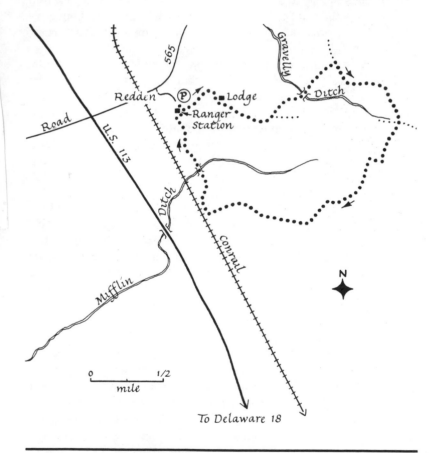

BIOLOGISTS GENERALLY RECOGNIZE SEVEN DIF-
ferent forest ecosystems in North America. Of these, the southeastern
Coastal Plain forest covers a comparatively small geographic area but
contains a rich array of tree species. This forest type is restricted to
the Atlantic seaboard from New Jersey south to Florida and continues
westward along the Gulf Coast to Texas, with a narrow band reaching
northward along the Mississippi Valley to southern Illinois. Pines cover
extensive parts of the forest, but oaks and hickories tend to dominate
sites free of fires. Hardwoods also are found in the wet lowlands.

Delaware's Redden State Forest contains good examples of trees
making up the Coastal Plain forest. Lying along the western edge of
the upland that splits the Delmarva Peninsula, the forest covers sandy
and remarkably flat land. Elevations average about forty-eight feet
above sea level and vary by only four feet over the entire length of
this hike. The trail is mostly on broad fire roads, but a short segment
follows the clearing along the forest boundary. This area is often wet,
so hiking boots are recommended.

The land was extensively farmed as recently as about fifty years ago,
but today the forest has reclaimed the old fields and few evidences of
man's agricultural practices can be found. Redden is by far the largest
of Delaware's three state forests. Managed primarily for timber production, the three thousand-acre forest also serves hunters, hikers,
naturalists, and other outdoor enthusiasts.

ACCESS

To reach the trailhead from Georgetown, drive west for 1.0 mile
on DE 18, then turn right (north) and continue for 3.0 miles on U.S.
113. Turn right on Road 565, pass through the tiny hamlet of Redden
at the railroad crossing, and then turn right into the entrance road to
Redden State Forest (0.5 mile from U.S. 113). Just 0.2 mile farther,
park your car on the left near the flagpole and office.

TRAIL

Walk along the entrance road, passing the ranger station and resi-
dence on the right. Just beyond, at a "T" intersection, turn left. You
will return to this spot along the right trail later in the hike. Pass
around a vehicle gate and continue along the wide, sandy forest road.

Around the bend you will pass in front of a large, rambling, wooden
building. Built by the Pennsylvania Railroad in 1903 as a hunting

97

lodge, the structure is still used today by organizations who rent it from the state. The rail line that brought train cars of quail hunters to Redden runs along the western boundary of the forest, but today only Conrail freight trains travel the tracks. When around the lodge, continue along the shady forest road.

At a fork, keep left on the more traveled road. Cross Gravelly Ditch on a wooden plank bridge. Walk around another vehicle gate and come upon a "T" intersection; turn right. The way passes by or through large tracts where lumbering has occurred; be alert to stay on the trail. A couple of old foundations, with trees growing in their centers and with moss-covered bricks now crumbling, can be seen along the right side of the trail. These remains are believed to be the ruins of farmhouses that once stood here.

Come upon a minor cross trail and keep straight. The forest road dead-ends at the boundary, marked by signs and horizontal yellow paint bands on trees; turn right and follow the cleared path along the property line. At a corner, identified by a concrete marker post painted yellow, turn left and continue to follow the cleared boundary. This area is swampy during wet seasons. The state land has been extensively logged; keep straight along the edge of the timbered area where the boundary clearing veers slightly left to cut a swath through the trees. You will very shortly come upon another forest road. By continuing about another two miles, you will complete the loop and be back at your car. This stretch is more scenic because most of the cutover areas are left behind and the wide road passes beneath a shady canopy of mixed hardwoods and evergreens, crossing Mifflin Ditch on a wood bridge. Gentians bloom along the edge of the trail in late summer and early autumn.

Trap Pond
State Park

Around a former millpond in
Delaware's oldest state park

Hiking distance: 4¾ miles
Hiking time: 2½ hours
Maps: USGS Trap Pond; park map

TRAP IS ONE OF THE MOST PICTURESQUE OF DELA-
ware's many millponds. Surrounded for the most part by thick forests,
the pond lies in a quiet, rural area. More species of trees are found
here than in any other comparable area in Delaware. The trees probably
of most interest to visitors are the baldcypresses, growing profusely
along most of the pond's margins and forming a dense swamp near
the headwaters. The cypress swamp can be seen best by boat or canoe,
but hikers on the trail described here also enjoy fine views. The Trap
Pond watershed harbors one of the northernmost stands of baldcypress
in the country. Most of the original baldcypress forest was cut in the
late 1700s so that, today, the oldest trees are slightly less than two
hundred years old and most are considerably younger. Some notable
specimens approach five feet in diameter. Other trees seen along the
trail include at least twelve different species of oak (blackjack, black,
white, swamp white, red, scarlet, water, willow, Spanish, pin, post,
and basket), four different species of pine (loblolly, scrub, pitch, and
shortleaf), American holly, American chestnut, tulip tree, beech, big-
tooth aspen, sweetgum, blackgum, red maple, pignut hickory, persim-
mon, sweetbay magnolia, and many others. A multitude of different
shrubs and small trees make up the understory. Herbaceous plants are
also diverse and numerous; moccasin-flower and netted chain fern are
two noteworthy examples.

In addition to the varied flora, the hiker has good opportunities to
see some of the park's wildlife. Turtles, water snakes, and frogs are
common in and around the pond. Squirrels (both red and eastern
gray), eastern chipmunks, eastern cottontails, and other small mam-

99

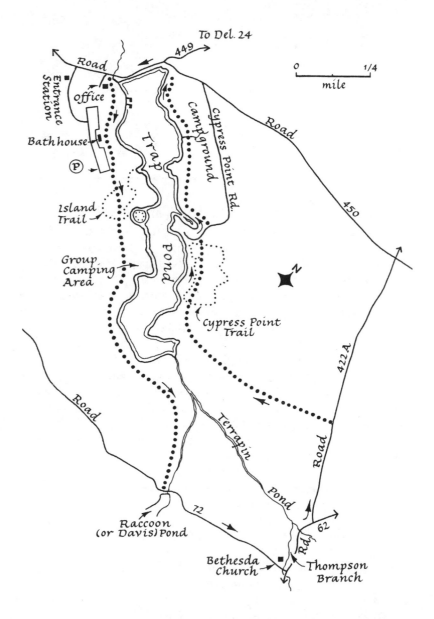

To Del. 24

449

0   1/4
mile

Road

Entrance Station

Office

Bathhouse

P

Island Trail

Group Camping Area

Trap

Pond

Campground

Cypress Point Rd.

Road

450

N

422 A

Road

Cypress Point Trail

Road

Terrapin

Pond

Raccoon (or Davis) Pond

72

62

Rd.

Bethesda Church

Thompson Branch

100

mals abound. Typical woodland birds are scarlet tanager, rufous-sided towhee, eastern kingbird, catbird, yellowthroat, wood thrush, common flicker, and bobwhite. Anglers fish Trap for bass, pickeral, bluegill, crappie, catfish, and perch.

The ninety-acre pond was created about 1790 to power a grist mill and a sawmill. In 1952, Trap Pond became Delaware's first state park. Our trail circumnavigates the pond in a counterclockwise direction, beginning and ending near the beach. A swim is always a good way to end a warm-weather hike, but a walk around Trap can be rewarding at any time of the year. In May, swamp azaleas, moccasin-flowers, and other spring plants are in bloom. Starting in May and extending into June, mountain laurel puts on a spectacular floral display. In the autumn, the earth glitters with leaves of the hardwoods and baldcypresses. Flowers of witch hazel burst forth in November. The park is largely deserted by people in the winter, and park roads may be closed to vehicular traffic after snowfalls. However, the trails remain open, and the hiker may see baldcypresses locked in ice — an unlikely setting for a cypress swamp! Any remaining open water in the middle of the pond is often crowded with whistling swans, Canada and snow geese, mallards, and American black ducks. On sunny winter days, the buckling, shifting ice breaks the silence with deep groans and eerie squeaks that seem to reverberate from shore to shore.

Other walks that can be enjoyed here cover the park's two nature trails, totaling 1¼ miles. Numbered posts along the trails correspond to descriptions in brochures available from park rangers or at the entrance station.

ACCESS

Trap Pond is near Laurel in southern Delaware. From downtown Laurel, head east for 5.3 miles on DE 24, turn right onto Road 449, and enter the park after 0.9 mile. Continue for another 0.3 mile, crossing the outlet from Trap Pond and then turning left onto the main entrance road. After the entrance station, you will come upon the first of two large parking lots that serve the picnic area and swimming beach. Turn right, drive past the bathhouse, and enter another large lot. Drive to the far end and park your car near the pond.

TRAIL

Facing the pond, you will see on your right a broad woods road that heads southeasterly through the forest. Turn and walk down the road. Just as you enter the woods, the Island Nature Trail loops from the right on its return to the trailhead. Shortly beyond, you intersect this trail again as it crosses our path. A few baldcypresses are visible in the low area on the left.

Continue straight, coming upon a primitive group camping area on the shore after about one-half mile. The trail passes through the camping area and stays near the water, affording occasional vistas of the pond studded with baldcypress trees.

About one-half mile from the group camping area, our trail reaches the headwaters of Trap Pond and turns right gradually, skirting a swampy lowland. Baldcypresses are mingled with other trees and brush in the swamp. Come out upon paved Road 72 and turn left.

The road very shortly bridges one of the inlets to Trap Pond. Raccoon, or Davis, Pond is on the right. Hike along the road for slightly more than one-half mile. The Bethesda Methodist Episcopal Church, a small, white, wooden structure built in 1878, is pleasantly set beneath tall trees by the side of the road.

Cross Thompson Branch, another inlet to Trap Pond, and immediately come upon a "T" junction with paved Road 62. Turn left and cross Terrapin Pond, a small creek that probably was a former millpond. Today no evidence of the pond remains, but the name persists. Fork left at the first opportunity onto gravel Road 422A. After about one-third mile, turn left off the road onto a woods road blocked with a chain strung between three posts. The entrance is marked by an iridescent warning triangle and by signs that read "Notice — No Hunting — State Park Area." Keep straight on the woods road, passing between a field of young pines and deciduous shrubs on the right and a more mature, mixed evergreen-hardwood forest on the left. The young pine plantation is soon left behind, and the trail becomes canopied by tall trees.

Continue on the broad woods road. The narrow Cypress Point Nature Trail eventually crosses our path. The nature trail is soon encountered again as it angles in from the left rear; Trap Pond comes into view on the left in this vicinity. The two trails run together for a short distance before the Cypress Point Trail veers left to remain close to the shore. Keep straight on the woods road. A little farther, a spur from the Cypress Point Trail designed for handicapped visitors comes in from the left and follows the woods road. Just beyond, the main Cypress Point Trail enters along an open area from the right, jogs onto the

102

Hoarfrost frames a trailside plant at Trap Pond.

woods road to intersect with the handicapped spur, and then turns left into the forest to return to the trailhead. Continue straight, and you will very soon pass around a chain barrier and come out onto paved Cypress Point Road. To the left, the road soon dead-ends at Cypress Point on Trap Pond, a site for primitive group camping.

Turn right and follow the road as it curves to the left. Just beyond the curve, turn left off the road onto a broad trail framed by two short posts and also marked by a white post with a black arrow pointing down the path. The trail follows a utility right-of-way and enters the park's campground.

Once in the campground, continue to follow the utility line, crossing a small cove on a wood bridge. Beyond the bridge, angle left and stay close to the shore. The trail is picked up again on the other side of the campground, entering the woods just to the left of campsite 16. The entrance has a wood pole placed across it to keep out vehicles. After about four hundred feet, the trail comes out at a boat ramp and then angles onto Road 450. Turn left on Road 450 and immediately left again onto Road 449.

The road crosses the dam that impounds Trap Pond. On the other side of the bridge over the outlet, descend the steps to the left and follow the shoreline back to the parking lot. The park office will be on your right, and you will walk past the boat rental concession stand, bathhouse, swimming beach, and picnic area.

Blackwater National Wildlife Refuge

Two easy walks in superb wildlife habitats.

Hiking distance: ¾ mile
Hiking time: ¾ hour
Maps: USGS Blackwater River; refuge map

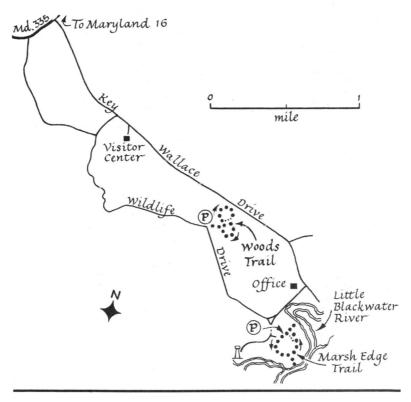

Md.335 — To Maryland 16

Key

Visitor Center

Wallace

Wildlife

Drive

P

Woods Trail

Drive

Office

Little Blackwater River

P

Marsh Edge Trail

N

0 — mile — 1

THE VAST MARSHES THAT LINE THE EASTERN shore of Chesapeake Bay reach the peak of their quiet beauty in southern Dorchester County, Maryland. The coast collapses in a mass of marshes and estuaries, and isolated towns lie at the end of long, flat roads. The colorful names of the curling waterways that lace this muddy lowland describe the slow, swampy nature of the watershed: Tedious Creek, Transquaking River, Backgarden Creek, Blackwater River. Topographic relief is so slight here that the Blackwater and its tributary the Little Blackwater arise within a stone's throw of large estuaries, yet they meander away from the shore, snaking southward through the marshes for miles before finally entering the Chesapeake at Fishing Bay.

The scenic heart of this waterlogged land has been set aside as Blackwater National Wildlife Refuge. The refuge is home to an astounding array of birds and mammals. The migrant life is especially rich. Among the birds, waterfowl are the most numerous residents. By late autumn, from 60,000 to 100,000 Canada geese can be counted during normal days. At the same time, well over 10,000 ducks representing twenty or more species will be spread out over the ponds and creeks. The duck population has declined in recent years not only at Blackwater but throughout the Atlantic flyway due to diminished habitat and loss of aquatic plants for food. From a peak of 191,000 in 1957, duck numbers have dropped to no more than 58,000 a year at Blackwater during the last decade.

Waterfowl may be the refuge's best known residents, but the rarer specics make Blackwater an extraordinary place for nature study. It is probably the best place in Maryland to see Delmarva fox squirrels and bald eagles. Over four hundred of the endangered squirrels live here, one of the largest of the five known relic populations remaining in Maryland and Virginia. They can sometimes be seen foraging on the ground at the edges of fields. About twenty bald eagles nest at Blackwater, the greatest nesting density of bald eagles in the eastern United States outside of Florida; from the windows of the visitor center it is not unusual to see an eagle perching on a snag or sailing above the marsh. In addition, the red-cockaded woodpecker, Maryland's rarest bird, has been seen at Blackwater a few times this century.

The refuge was established in 1932 as a resting and feeding place for migratory waterfowl. Like the other Delmarva wildlife refuges, it consists mostly of tidal marsh. The marsh is a complex, fragile landscape whose existence is dependent on definite, specific water levels.

Of course, the daily tides are the heartbeat of the marsh and are essential to its well-being, but extended periods of high water can kill or injure the unique plants that constitute the marsh. Low water is just as damaging. The Blackwater marshes are being pressured by diverse factors and have experienced a long decline. In 1933, the refuge enclosed roughly 10,000 acres of marsh. Today, only about 4,300 acres remain.

This frighteningly huge loss is thought to have many causes, ranging from man-made influences such as fires and road building to overgrazing by wildlife, especially geese and muskrats. Evidence also points to causes far more inexorable. The coast crumbles before the relentless tide for, in the push and pull of the waves, there is slightly more land lost than gained. The entire Delmarva Peninsula appears to be slowly sinking; the water level in Chesapeake Bay has apparently risen about three feet in the last three hundred years. The gradual encroachment of water may be a natural process that will continue to claim marshland.

Management practices at the refuge are devoted to waterfowl protection and enhancement, and waterfowl need the marsh. The refuge managers, alarmed at the loss of such prime habitat, decided to attack the endless mutation of the coast head-on: they are building new marsh. The scheme shows some success; about fifteen to thirty acres are restored each year. The goal is to create a buffer of marsh across open water that will intercept storm winds and waves. In addition to providing new, man-made feeding areas for waterfowl, such a barrier will help protect several islands of loblolly pines where eagles nest.

The Blackwater Refuge consists of more than fourteen thousand acres, but only a few dozen are open to the foot-borne traveler. Some additional areas can be seen from your car only. You cannot walk on fields or marsh or along Wildlife Drive. A management principle at Blackwater states that wildlife should be disturbed as little as possible. The birds here are more comfortable with automobiles than with humans; you will likely see more wildlife by staying in your car because it serves as a blind. Nevertheless, two short, separate trails have been built in different habitats of the refuge so that visitors can sample this environment on foot. These are the two trails described here, and they are ideal for families with small children. Dogs are permitted if on a leash. I recommend repellent in the warmer months and binoculars at any time of the year. A variety of wildlife can be seen during all seasons; the best time for viewing waterfowl is between mid-October and mid-March.

The boardwalk on the Marsh Edge Trail enables hikers to experience firsthand the great marsh that lines the Little Blackwater River.

ACCESS

From Cambridge, drive southwest on MD 16. After 7.1 miles, in the village of Church Creek, turn left (south) onto MD 335. Follow the signs to the refuge, turning left onto Key Wallace Drive in 3.7 miles. The visitor center appears on the right after 1.0 mile. Pamphlets, maps, species lists, restrooms, water, and observation windows are provided here. Another 1.6 miles beyond the visitor center on Key Wallace Drive is the refuge office on the right; turn right onto Wildlife

108

Drive. Just 0.2 mile farther, fork left, and then turn left in 0.1 mile into the trailhead parking lot.

TRAILS

Our first walk is along the Marsh Edge Trail, one-third mile long, and begins in a mixed hardwood-evergreen forest. Loblolly pine, sweetgum, various oaks, and American holly are some of the trees that can be seen here. The path is covered with wood chips and is bordered with cut branches and logs. It soon leads to the edge of the marsh that lines the Little Blackwater River; wooden benches here and elsewhere invite you to sit while observing wildlife or contemplating the landscape. An osprey nesting platform (vacant during my last visit) stands in the marsh.

A little farther, an eighty-foot boardwalk extends over the marsh to open water. After the boardwalk spur, the trail remains in the woods. At a fork, keep right, walk through a young pine forest, and you will soon come upon a clearing with two trails diverging from the far side. Take the right path that leads shortly to a viewpoint over the water, then return to the clearing and follow the other path directly to the parking lot.

Once back in your car, a turn to the left out of the parking lot leads shortly to an observation tower overlooking the junction of the Blackwater and Little Blackwater rivers and their marshlands. To drive directly to our next trail, turn right out of the lot, retrace your route 1.0 mile to Wildlife Drive, turn left, and go 0.7 mile to a parking area on the right.

The one-half mile Woods Trail loops through a mature upland forest of pine and mixed hardwoods, prime habitat for the beleaguered Delmarva fox squirrel. This path is also covered with wood chips and bordered by logs and branches. Benches enable you to sit quietly and observe the life of the forest. Along the trail you will find old drainage ditches, furrows, and rusting machinery — evidence that this land was once farmed.

Just beyond the trail entrance, fork left. A little farther, a side path to the right provides a shortcut to the return loop. The main trail continues and soon circles back to your car. Drive along the one-way Wildlife Drive to return to the visitor center or MD 335.

Wicomico
Demonstration
Forest

A network of logging roads, old woods roads, and firebreaks through upland forest

Hiking distance: 3 miles
Hiking time: 1½ hours
Map: USGS Wango

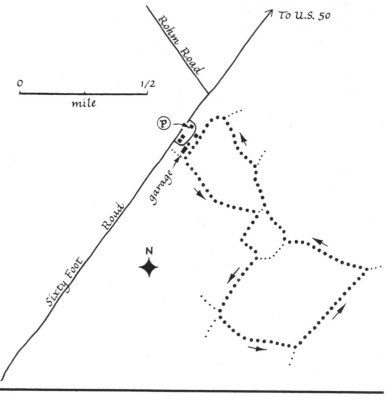

To U.S. 50

Rohm Road

0   1/2
mile

P

garage

Sixty Foot Road

N

WICOMICO IS ANOTHER OF THE SMALL MARYLAND forests whose status was changed to "demonstration forest" in 1983. The sign at the headquarters on Sixty Foot Road still says "Wicomico State Forest." The trees in the forest are also still sold and cut by lumber companies to produce revenue for the operation of the overall state forest system, but the management emphasis is now shifting to the development of Wicomico as a specific forest demonstration area and educational training site.

A study for Wicomico's latest management plan shows that 90 percent of the public use of the forest occurs during deer hunting week. A few other hunters are afield during bow season and small game season. Only an occasional hiker or nature lover visits Wicomico during the entire rest of the year, the perfect time, then, to schedule your walk. If you are lucky enough to avoid loggers (who usually do not work on weekends), you will likely find a peaceful quietness in the forest, a natural stillness punctuated only by the hum of insects, the call of birds, and the quiet whisper of wind through the loblolly pines.

All three of the thrushes that overwinter on the Delmarva Peninsula seem to favor the thick undergrowth of the forest. I saw eastern bluebirds, American robins, and hermit thrushes during my hike in February.

ACCESS

From Salisbury, drive east on U.S. 50 for 9.8 miles to Sixty Foot Road. Turn right (MD 353 goes to the left at this intersection). After 1.8 miles, you will come upon the forest headquarters complex on the left. Turn into the U-shaped drive and leave your car in the small parking area behind the middle building on the inner loop.

TRAIL

Walk along the drive in the direction of the large, cinder-block garage and shop on the outer loop. Turn left off the drive just before reaching the garage, walk through the shop yard, and pick up our trail behind the building. The path to the left is our return. For now, turn right, and soon you will cross a ditch running along the edge of the maintenance yard. Just beyond, you will come upon a "T" intersection; turn left, following the main trail.

You will shortly encounter another "T" intersection. The connecting trail to the left leads, in just a few steps, to our return loop (visible

111

coming in from the right of the connecting path). Turn right to continue our hike, staying on the broad, main trail. After curving sharply to the left, you will come upon yet another "T" junction as you face a recently timbered area ahead. Turn right, keeping the logged tract on your left. (Going to the left here would lead again to our return loop.)

About one mile into the hike, you will come upon a major trail intersection — turn left, staying on the most traveled trail. Our path curves sharply to the left where a more minor trail enters from the right. The straight path you are now traveling runs along the boundary of the state land; the forest on the right is in private ownership. As you come upon a gate across a trail leading to a paved road, turn sharply left and walk along a firebreak.

The trail broadens into a logging road as you come to a timbered area on the left. As the road curves to the left, turn right onto a less-traveled woods road. (Continuing on the logging road would bring you to the entrance loop.) You will soon come upon a "T" intersection, the trail to the left leading immediately to your original entrance path. Go right on the woods road to complete the return loop.

After forking left, you will come to a "T" junction. Turn left. The trail soon returns to the headquarters complex. Continue straight, following the path behind the buildings until you come upon a road to the right leading into the maintenance yard and to the parking area.

Pocomoke State Forest

A network of wide, level trails in the Pocomoke River watershed

Hiking distance: 4¼ miles
Hiking time: 2 hours
Maps: USGS Snow Hill; forest map

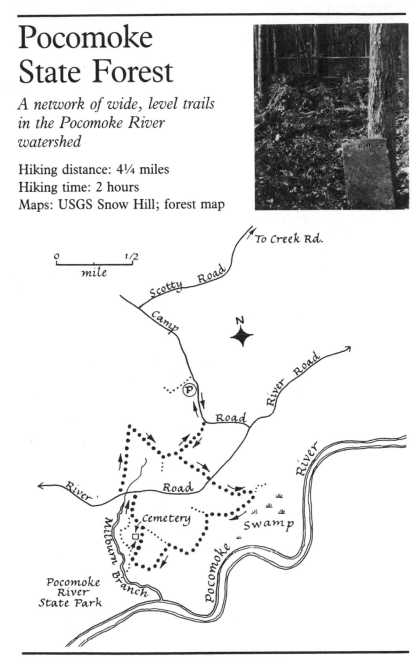

THE UPLAND AREAS OF WHAT IS NOW POCOMOKE

State Forest were devoted to agriculture from the days of early settlement until the 1920s. Some of the plowed furrows can still be seen, now lying in thick forests. Diminishing crop yields, depleted soil, and economic hardships forced many people off farms in the 1930s, and the land was abandoned. Governments stepped in to set up soil conservation measures and to provide forest fire protection. Two Civilian Conservation Corps camps were established. The old fields reverted to pure stands of loblolly pine from natural seeding. Most of Maryland's timber income is derived from loblolly pine, and today the former farmlands are providing wood fibre for products such as saw logs, poles, piling, basket veneer, and pulpwood. The trail described here traverses clearcut areas, allowing you to observe how loblolly pines fuel Maryland's modern timbering industry.

The most obvious signs of the people once living here are the old cemeteries they left behind. Scattered through the forest and victim of neglect and vandalism, the small family burial plots are reminders of the changing patterns of land use. This hike passes by a quiet, nineteenth-century graveyard.

The trail additionally skirts the dense Pocomoke River swamp. Early settlers considered the swamp virtually impenetrable and only made forays into it to cut the most valuable baldcypress trees. In the mid-1800s, the river and its swamps became a link in the Underground Railroad; escaping slaves and their abolitionist guides followed the river north to Delaware and eventually to the safety and freedom of Pennsylvania. Some two thousand slaves beat their way north along the Railroad on the Eastern Shore. Untold numbers died in the swamps, drowned in the rivers, or were recaptured by bounty hunters. During the Civil War, the swamp became notorious as a hideout for smugglers, bootleggers, outlaws, and deserters. After the war, as things returned to normal and technology improved, even the swamp forest became accessible to lumbermen and most of the trees were cut down.

The trailhead is on a little hillock, elevation thirty feet. The trail drops very gradually to less than five feet along the swamp. The woods roads and fire roads this hike follows generally are only mowed once a year. At times they become overgrown with rank vegetation. Repellent is de rigueur under these conditions. During certain times, tick populations reach excessively high levels and voracious mosquitoes lie in wait at the edge of the swamp. Hunting is allowed throughout the forest; planning your visit to avoid hunting season will add to your safety.

114

ACCESS

From Snow Hill, go north on MD 12 for 2.8 miles. Turn left on Red House Road. After 1.2 miles you will cross Nassawango Creek on a plank bridge and immediately will come upon a fork. Bear left onto Creek Road, drive 0.2 mile, and then fork right onto Scotty Road. Continue for 3.0 miles to where Scotty Road makes a 90° turn to the right. Camp Road, narrow, dirt, and seldom traveled, goes off to the left. Turn onto Camp Road and soon you will enter the state forest, although the boundary is unmarked. Follow Camp Road for 0.6 mile and park on the right where a woods road enters. This spot is the only place along Camp Road with space enough for a parked car. Be sure not to block access to the woods road. (If coming from Salisbury, drive southeast on MD 12 for 14.4 miles, turn right onto Red House Road, and then follow the above directions.)

TRAIL

Walk south on Camp Road for one-third mile. If you are here in September or October, look for the delicate blue flowers of downy gentians on the shoulders of Camp Road and along sandy stretches of the woods trails. When the road veers sharply to the left, keep straight (right) on a fire road. Walk for about another one-fourth mile until you come to a large clearcut area. The fire road makes a sharp left turn as a logging road angles in from the right through the timbered area. This logging path is your return loop. The fire road goes southeasterly with the clearcut on the right for about one-fourth mile, and then crosses paved River Road.

South of the road the trail passes through a young forest (mostly pines on the left and mostly hardwoods on the right), and begins a very gradual descent to the Pocomoke River bottomland. Farther along, the trees are larger and are characterized by sweetgum, tulip tree, and a variety of oaks. You will come to a "T" junction after about one-fourth mile. Turn right on the woods road, paralleling the Pocomoke River swamp.

Follow the woods road, which keeps to higher ground along the edge of the swamp. At places to the left you can see the steep bank that drops to the bottomland. The suffusive greens of the baldcypresses stand out among the red maples, black gums, and other swamp-loving plants. The trail is straight except for a broad, U-shaped loop that

115

goes around a tongue of swampland. Pass a side trail forking to the right on the loop. Beyond, the trail turns sharply to the right, away from the swamp, and soon comes to the edge of a timbered tract. Avoid the cutover area by forking left on a trail that follows the edge of the forest.

The trail turns sharply right at the boundary with Pocomoke River State Park, marked by "No Hunting" signs. Further, at a major trail junction, turn right, and then keep right at the fork walking slightly uphill. The trail to the left leads to the state park and the fork to the left continues along the boundary line.

Near the top of the small rise, the old Bevans cemetery is nestled in an overgrown tangle of trees, shrubs, ferns, and honeysuckle. The thickets, aided by vandals, have nudged the weathered, gray tombstones into rakish slants. Other stones in the plot are toppled over, broken off, or leaning against trees. All the graves list burial dates in the first half of the nineteenth century; the earliest I could find was of Priscella Bevans, who died April 23, 1828.

Beyond the graveyard, the trail enters a timbered area and is much overgrown with tall bush-clovers, grasses, and other plants. Watch closely for a "T" junction in the midst of the cutover tract and turn left. The trail soon clears and comes once again to the boundary with the state park at another "T" junction. Turn right (north) and walk through forestland to River Road. There, turn left (west), cross Milburn Branch, and then turn right (north) on a woods road just beyond a game food plot. You will pass more food plots scattered through this forest.

The trail reaches the edge of state land after about one-half mile, when it encounters a fence line and agricultural fields. Make a sharp turn on the trail to the right rear and stay in the woods. Walk about one-fourth mile until you come out into a large cutover tract near a lone, tall loblolly pine. The woods road continues, but turn left on a logging road and follow the curving edge of the lumbered area (on your right) and the forest (on your left). This logging road soon meets the fire road you traversed early in the hike. A turn to the left (northeast) will take you back to Camp Road and your vehicle.

Baldcypress Nature Trail

A nature walk in Pocomoke River State Park

Hiking distance: 1 mile
Hiking time: ¾ hour
Maps: USGS Girdletree and Snow
  Hill; park map

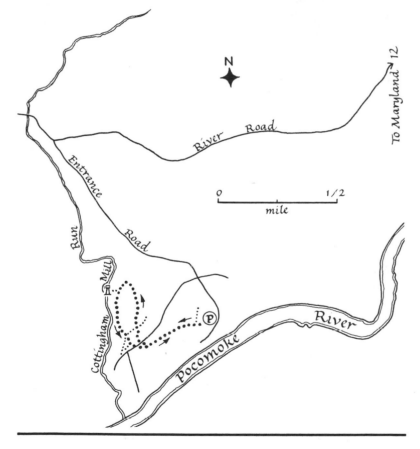

MARYLAND IS THE ONLY STATE IN WHICH BOTH

American larch and baldcypress occur naturally. These two trees are the only conifers in North America that shed their leaves in the autumn. The needles of both turn to a beautiful yellowish brown before falling. Both species are typical inhabitants of wetlands, but here their similarities end. American larch, or tamarack, is a northern species, found as far north as the Arctic timber line. In the contiguous United States, it is restricted to cold northern or high mountain bogs where extreme acidity of soil and water permit only certain specialized plants to grow. One such bog is found in the high Alleghenies of far western Maryland.

On the other hand, baldcypress is a southern tree, growing majestically in lowland swamps of the Coastal Plain and along streams and rivers throughout the South. To many people, mature stands of baldcypress draped with Spanish moss represent the primeval nature of the southern swamps. The Maryland populations of baldcypress occur sporadically in several bottomland habitats, most notably along the Pocomoke River. The Pocomoke, from its headwaters in Delaware's Cypress Swamp to its mouth at Pocomoke Sound, is lined with baldcypress.

The wood of baldcypress is prized by lumbermen because it is highly resistant to decay. Early settlers along the Pocomoke began logging the swamp and used the baldcypress for shipbuilding, shingles, siding on homes, water tanks, and coffins. The Pocomoke River swamp forest had been completely timbered by the 1930s when the federal government began acquiring abandoned land in the watershed. The state assumed control of this land in 1954. With protection, the swamp forest is returning to a more natural state. It will be many years before the baldcypress again dominates the swamp; baldcypress is very slow to regenerate second-growth stands because small trees are shaded by the swamp hardwoods. But it is, after all, the supreme tree of the rich river swamps, and young baldcypresses are making a comeback.

Pocomoke River State Park preserves some of the finest second-growth stands of baldcypress. The trail described here, in the Milburn Landing area of the park, brings the hiker to the edge of the baldcypress swamp, passing through other forest types as well. None of the trees here are wreathed with Spanish moss (that plant drops out in southern Virginia), nor has the cutover baldcypress forest regained its lofty maturity; yet, the essence of the swamp persists — dark, still, dense, trackless, inscrutable.

118

This easy walk is well suited for families with young children. Dogs must be on a leash. A leaflet, describing the numbered stations along the way, is available from rangers or at the trailhead. The park map inaccurately shows the trailway for the Baldcypress Nature Trail, although the trailhead parking area is correctly depicted. Bring insect repellent.

ACCESS

Milburn Landing was formerly a separate state park. In 1975, it was joined with Shad Landing State Park on the south bank of the Pocomoke to form the new Pocomoke River State Park. Some road signs, old maps, and local residents still refer to it as "Milburn Landing State Park." From Snow Hill, drive north on MD 12 for 1.2 miles. Turn left at the flashing caution light onto Nassawango Road. (MD 354 goes right at this intersection.) Drive for 2.2 miles, crossing the broad Nassawango Creek on a plank bridge, and fork left onto River Road where Creek Road goes right. Continue on River Road for 4.3 miles and turn left into Pocomoke River State Park. Follow the entrance road straight for 1.0 mile and turn right into the dirt parking lot. Leave your car by the "Baldcypresss Nature Trail" sign. (If coming from Salisbury, drive southeast on MD 12 for 16.1 miles, turn right onto Nassawango Road, and then follow the above directions.)

TRAIL

Walk past the sign and enter a grove of loblolly pines. Pass a side trail leading to the youth group camping area to the right.

The loblollies are soon left behind and the trail wanders through a mixed hardwood forest of maples, tulip tree, sweetgum, oaks, and other species. After station 8, fork right; you will return to this spot along the left fork. Cross the paved park road and continue straight.

After station 10, you will encounter a cross trail. (If you want to shorten your walk, a turn to the left here soon brings you to the return loop of the Baldcypress Nature Trail.) The path ahead shortly reaches the Pocomoke River swamp and skirts the edge of the swamp for one-fourth mile. In the late summer and autumn, the rich humus along the edge of the swamp is a good place to find Indian-pipe and pinesap, small saprophytic plants of the wintergreen family that lack chlorophyll.

119

A short spur leads from the main trail along an old road to an observation deck overlooking Cottingham Mill Branch (also called Cottingham Mill Run). This creek is representative of the myriad small waterways that course through the swamp, convoluted and choked with chaotic plant growth.

Return to the main trail, turn right, and you will soon reenter the mixed hardwood forest. Just beyond station 23, pass the shortcut trail and then another side trail to the right.

Again cross the park road, and very shortly you will intersect with the path leading back to the parking area.

Janes Island State Park

Boat excursion and beach walking along a wild Chesapeake shore

Hiking distance: 3 or 4 miles, depending on side trail
Hiking time: 1½-2 hours
Maps: USGS Marion, Terrapin Sand Point, and Great Fox Island

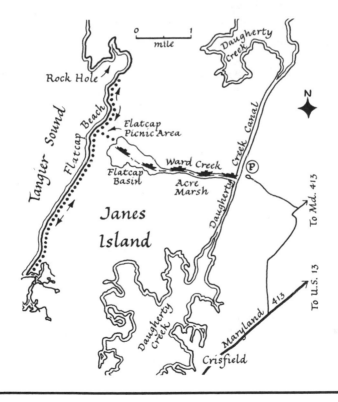

JANES ISLAND IS ONLY A STONE'S THROW FROM the mainland, yet, like all islands, a feeling of remoteness and inaccessibility soon surrounds its human visitors. The sweep of its marshes offers vistas across miles of waving grasses. The grand marshes, sandy beaches, shallow salt flats, small, upland hummocks, coves, and ponds are abundant with avian life and teeming with marine creatures, such as tiny scuds less than one-eighth inch long, big blue crabs over seven inches across, prize black drum that tip the scales at eighty-six pounds, and the "most celebrated of American turtles," the diamondback terrapin.

The eastern edge of the island's marsh was ditched and dredged by the United States Army Corps of Engineers in 1939 to create the narrow Dougherty Creek Canal. The channel is also called the Annemessex Canal because it connects the Big Annemessex River along the northern shore of Janes Island with the Little Annemessex River that curves around the island's southern end. The canal offers fishing boats from nearby waters a shortcut for bringing their daily catch of seafood to Crisfield.

Crisfield, a small town of 2,900, describes itself as the "Seafood Capital of the World." It is at least undisputably the leading blue crab port of the Atlantic coast. The southern half of Janes Island forms part of Crisfield's harbor. The island was the site of one of the town's seafood processing plants early this century, the boom years when entrepreneurs shipped 125 million pounds of oysters out of the port annually. Downtown Crisfield is built on about six feet of oyster shells, the residues from the first shucking houses in the late 1800s.

Today, Crisfield is best known for Atlantic blue crab. The Chesapeake Bay provides more crabs for human consumption than any other body of water in the world (some 66 million pounds a year), and Tangier Sound, which Janes Island faces on the west, is the part of the bay where most of those crabs are captured. This area is the heart of the Chesapeake.

Chesapeake means "great shellfish bay" in the original Indian language. Through the ages, many shamans, sages, poets, philosophers, and other writers have discoursed enthusiastically on the Chesapeake. An early settler described it as "the Noblest Bay in the Universe." H.L. Mencken called it a "great big outdoor protein factory." Eastern Shore poet Albert Dowling wrote:

122

Yet I have loved one spot on earth, one part
Of God's good world beyond the power to speak,
Remembered well and kept in grateful heart
My native shores along the Chesapeake.

The bay's grandeur, quiet beauty, fecundity, and life-sustaining qualities place it prominently on the list of earth's superlatives. It is 195 miles long, 3 to 35 miles wide, and has between 4,600 and 5,100 miles of shoreline (estimates vary). It is North America's largest and most productive estuary and one of the largest and most productive estaurine systems in the world. The Chesapeake is obviously of immense economic importance to Maryland, Virginia, and neighboring coastal states because of its fishing and recreational value, but it is also absolutely essential to the multitudes of wildlife that live all or part of their lives in the water or on the shore. The bay is the spawning, nursery, or feeding grounds for one hundred species of fish. Between 500,000 and 800,000 waterfowl can be found overwintering on the Chesapeake. The threatened osprey is more common around the bay than anywhere else in the United States, and bald eagles nest along its shore.

Marshy Janes Island, with its luxuriant forests of tall grasses, its curling creeks, and its muddy flats, is typical of the delicately balanced ecosystems in the bay. Such marshland ranks among the most organically productive areas on earth, often supporting more life per acre than the richest farmland. The low, flat island represents landscape reduced to its essentials — surface, horizon, and sky. The highest elevation is only seven feet above sea level. Janes is an idyllic spot to watch the antics of gulls, enjoy the afternoon sun, or trace the patterns of clouds in the wide, mirrored sky.

The island, however, is not without its difficulties during certain times of the year. Visitors to Janes must be prepared to cope with ravenous greenheads, so-called because of the large, iridescent, green eyes covering most of the head. After being bitten by one of these big horse flies, you may think the rest of the head is devoted to piercing mouthparts, which it pretty much is. The island is one of the orneriest places on the Delmarva Peninsula for biting insects.

Janes Island State Park consists of two areas — a small, mainland portion (the Hodson Memorial Area, with roads, campground, boat ramp, picnic area, playground, and other amenities) and Janes Island itself, a three thousand-acre natural area almost totally undeveloped.

123

No designated trails exist in the park; the hike described here follows the western shoreline of Janes, fronting Tangier Sound. Dogs are prohibited from all parts of the state park.

ACCESS

To reach Janes Island State Park from Princess Anne, drive south 1.3 miles on MD 675. Continue south (left) on U.S. 13 for 3.4 miles to the junction with MD 413. Turn right (south). After 10.9 miles turn right on an unnamed road in the little village of Hopewell; this side road is marked with a sign pointing right to "Airport." Airport Road goes to the right after 0.6 mile at a point where our road makes a sharp turn to the left. After another 0.8 mile, turn right at an intersection with a sign pointing to the state park. Enter the Hodson Memorial Area of the park in 0.5 mile. Continue straight past the campground roads to the picnic area/playground parking lot.

Catch the *Osprey*, the Maryland Park Service's pontoon ferry, at the dock on the Dougherty Creek Canal. Fare is 75¢ for adults and 50¢ for children round trip. The boat runs every day except Thursday from Memorial Day weekend to Labor Day. Departures from the mainland are on the hour from 1 to 5 p.m. Monday–Wednesday and Friday. On weekends and holidays, departures are on the hour from 10 a.m. to 5 p.m. Storms may force a change in the schedule. Call the park at 301-968-1565 for information.

The *Osprey* soon turns out of the canal and heads westward up Ward Creek into the middle of Janes Island. The creek drains Acre Marsh and widens into Flatcap Basin, one of the many ponds, big and small, dotting the interior of the island.

TRAIL

Disembark from the ferry, follow the long wharf to the shore, and make your way through the Flatcap Picnic Area, characterized by scattered clumps of sparse plants that have established footholds in the crusty salt pans and low sand dunes. A few, weathered picnic tables and two chemical toilets attest to the part-time presence of our fellow men.

Arrive at Flatcap Beach, a lovely, wide strand of fine sand sloping gently from a small front dune into the clear waters of Tangier Sound. Here is a fine swimming beach; the water is shallow and warm and little waves lap languidly against the shore. Much of the rest of the

124

shore on Janes facing the sound is interspersed with mud flats and thick stands of eelgrass.

Tangier Sound is separated loosely from the main body of the Chesapeake Bay by a string of low islands. From north to south, the islands are Bloodsworth, South Marsh, Smith, and Tangier. The last two are inhabited by watermen and their families. Tangier, in Virginia waters, contains about 850 people and is the most densely settled.

The sound is dotted with small white buoys marking crab pots lying on the bottom. A waterman may put out two hundred of the cubical pots, each weighing about eighteen pounds and made of very thin, treated, steel wire. The pots are baited with dead menhaden and must be checked every few days. Both the newly caught crabs and the menhaden in the pots probably began their lives in the marshes of Janes Island or in another wetland along the seaboard. The Atlantic menhaden, called alewife by the Chesapeake watermen, spawns in the open sea, but the salt marsh is a necessary part of their life cycle. Menhaden is the principal commercial fish of the East Coast but is a fish no one eats. Its oil is pressed out and used in the manufacture of paints, inks, soaps, and lubricants. The fish are processed, dried, and ground into meal for animal feed. A waterman will also consume bushels of them as bait in his crab pots.

Turn left (south) and walk along the curving shore. As Flatcap Beach is left behind, groves of submerged eelgrass occur just offshore. A ragged windrow of uprooted eelgrass lines the upper shore, left there along with the other flotsam by the high tide. Blue crabs and horseshoe crabs can be seen swimming in the sparkling water. The eelgrass beds are frequented by snowy egrets, little blue herons, and other waders in search of crabs and fish. Shells are everywhere; I found soft-shelled clams, razor clams, oysters, stout tagelus, and ribbed mussels. Driftwood, encrusted with rock barnacles and worn smooth by the journey through salt water and by subsequent sandblasting on the beach, litters the shore. The skyline of Crisfield is visible on the southeastern horizon; at midday the town's noon whistle can be heard, clear but faint across the water and marsh.

The beach narrows drastically and becomes a thin strip of sand between the mud flats of the sound and the foot-high dune backed by Janes' marshy interior. Hundreds of dragonflies, representing several species with a range of sizes and a remarkable diversity of brilliant colors, zip across the open wetland or rest on the tips of the marsh grasses. Boat-tailed grackles, red-winged blackbirds, marsh wrens, and seaside sparrows are the birds most commonly observed in the

125

marsh. I was not lucky enough to see any diamondback terrapins on the island, but I discovered many tracks across the soft sand where the turtles had crawled from the sound over to the marsh or vice versa. The tracks appear as two shallow, parallel furrows, with the tail dragging in between.

My disappointment over the lack of turtle sightings was lessened somewhat when I spotted a dunlin feeding on a mud flat. These sandpipers are fairly common in the lower Chesapeake in the winter, but this was late June! For some reason, this lone dunlin had tarried in Maryland before migrating to its tundra breeding grounds. Sightings like this, perhaps combined with a view of an osprey plunging into the sound and emerging with a fish grasped in its talons or of an oystercatcher picking up bivalves along the shore or of a harrier sweeping low over the marsh, make Janes Island very popular with birders.

I discovered a projectile point embedded halfway in the sand at the water's edge. Indian artifacts, ranging from points to scrapers to fire stones, are sometimes found on the shoreline. The Annemessex visited the island regularly to hunt, fish, and gather crabs and clams. Although unlikely that they lived on the island year-round, the abundance of game and other food obviously made it an important part of their tribal lands.

After about 1½ miles, you will reach the end of our trail at the edge of a deep, wide, swift-flowing tidal creek that drains the interior of the island through a break in the dune line. A tall chimney is visible far across the island to the south, the remains of a fish factory built on the southern side of Janes in 1880. All but the fifty-foot brick chimney was destroyed by fire in the 1930s. On a clear day, Smith Island is visible across Tangier Sound. Smith is actually a miniature archipelago; the marshy northern portion (the part visible from Janes) is Glen L. Martin National Wildlife Refuge, the more central section is home to three separate watermen communities, while the low-lying, uninhabited, southern part is in Virginia.

Turn and retrace your path to Flatcap Beach. To extend your hike on Janes Island, you can walk north from Flatcap Beach for about one-half mile to Rock Hole, a shallow, sleeping cove off Tangier Sound. From here, South Marsh Island, a mere shadow on the water, can be seen on a clear day across the sound. Appropriately named, uninhabited South Marsh is a very low-lying marshland, barely emerging above the waters of the bay; it is a state-owned wildlife management area.

Walk back to Flatcap Beach and to the dock in Flatcap Basin, and catch the *Osprey* to the mainland.

126

Delaware Bay/
Atlantic Ocean

Assateague Island

Blackbird
State Forest

*An upland forest walk featuring
Carolina bays*

Hiking distance: 6 miles
Hiking time: 3 hours
Map: USGS Clayton

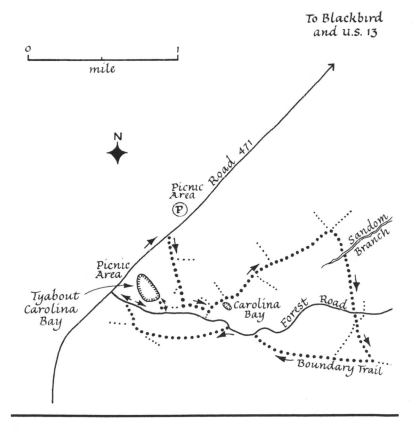

BLACKBIRD STATE FOREST CONSISTS OF FIVE SEPArate tracts in north-central Delaware. The largest of these, the Tyabout Tract, is the setting for this hike. Many areas of the Tyabout Tract are former cultivated fields replanted with pines. These groves of evergreens, now tall and stately, provide striking contrasts with the climax deciduous forest found on other portions of the state land. "Each pine is like a great green feather stuck in the ground," as Thoreau wrote in an 1851 entry in his *Journal*. Trees along this walk include Virginia pine, white pine, loblolly pine, red pine, tulip tree, sweetgum, black tupelo, white oak, willow oak, swamp white oak, dogwood, red maple, and several hickories.

This area is noted for the circular or elliptical depressions scattered throughout the wooded landscape. To a hiker attuned to changes in landforms and to subtle differences in vegetation, these oval lowlands command immediate attention; they are clearly unlike their surroundings. Called Carolina bays because of superficial similarities to other depressions first discovered in the Carolinas, these sinks may be as much as twenty feet below the encircling rim (although most are considerably shallower). Those in this area are sometimes more appropriately called Delmarva bays to distinguish them from those in the South.

The depressions are spectacular in a quiet sort of way. Much of their appeal lies in their unique biota and in their scattered but regular occurrence in small geographic areas. Their origin has defied explanation and remains a mystery. Lorraine Fleming, in *Delaware's Outstanding Natural Areas and Their Preservation*, points out the special character of these puzzling landforms:

> The origin of Carolina bays, also termed sinkholes, whale wallows, round ponds, black bottoms, and loblollies, is a subject of considerable controversy. A number of theories have been advanced, but not one has been adequately substantiated or widely accepted. An intriguing but implausible idea contends that whales were stranded by shallow receding seas and wallowed helplessly, thus creating the depressions. Others include ancient meteorite impact, the melting of stranded ice debris originating from Pleistocene glaciation, and the "water table-sinkhole-lacustrine-aeolian" theory, a two-phase geomorphic cycle in which a basin phase is fol-

lowed by a bay phase and finally drainage by stream incursion. Carolina bays are in every sense of the word geological and biological enigmas.

Several hundred Carolina bays were located in this part of Delaware and neighboring Maryland, all occurring within a fifty-mile radius and generally running in a diagonal southwest-northeast band. Most have been altered or destroyed by erosion, ditching, draining, cultivation, filling, or development. The few, undisturbed bays remaining are usually the deeper ones found in wooded areas. Recently recognized as unique natural treasures containing glade and swamp plant communities found nowhere else in the country, the unaltered bays are finally receiving protection. In 1984 the state of Delaware established the Blackbird Carolina Bays Nature Preserve within Blackbird State Forest to conserve the bays and their immediate surroundings in a natural state. In addition, the Nature Conservancy is acquiring several outstanding bays in Maryland for inclusion in their preserve system.

This hike passes by two fine examples of Carolina bays, nestled among trees and now protected from man-made changes. Carolina bays are poorly drained and many contain water throughout the year; thus, most hikers view them from the perimeter. They can perhaps be seen best in the winter, when the water may be absent or at least lowered and when the leaves are off the dense vegetation.

ACCESS

From Wilmington, drive south on U.S. 13 for 26.9 miles to the little community of Blackbird. Turn right on Road 471. Enter Blackbird State Forest after 1.6 miles. In another 0.5 mile you will see a small picnic area on the right. Park in the picnic area lot.

TRAIL

Cross Road 471 and turn right. Walk along the road for a short distance to the end of a thick grove of pines. Turn left onto a trail separating the pine grove on the left from a recently timbered tract on the right. The evergreen plantation was seeded in 1946–1947 with white, red, and loblolly pines to serve as a forest demonstration tract.

Keep right where a side trail comes in from the left out of the pines. The cutover area is left behind and the path wanders through an imposing grove of tall white pines. Fork left and come upon a "T"

131

intersection as you come out of the pines. Turn left, walking on a broad path between an evergreen forest on your left and a deciduous forest on your right. Our trail angles near a one-lane forest road but turns sharply left where a short side trail, blocked by a cable, goes right to intercept the road.

You will come upon another trail going both left and right. Turn right and immediately cross over a cable strung between two posts. Just beyond, you will enter a narrow forest road — turn right. The small tear-shaped lowland visible to the right during all these turns is a Carolina bay.

The forest road very soon turns sharply to the left, leaving the Carolina bay behind. The road separates a white pine tract (planted in 1960) on the left from hardwoods on the right. Continue on the road where a trail goes off to the right and, beyond, where a forest road leads left to the ranger station and office. Tall, spindly loblolly pines, also planted in 1960, replace the white pines on the left.

Where the loblolly pines end, a minor cross trail is encountered. Turn right, descend very slightly, and cross Sandom Beach as best you can. Beyond the stream, the broad path climbs gently and passes through mature oaks and hickories in a secluded section of the forest. I found the old skull of a red fox at the base of a willow oak near the trail.

Cross diagonally the one-lane forest road you saw early in the hike. Just beyond the road, a cross trail comes in. Continue straight to a "T" junction with a boundary trail that runs along the perimeter of state land. Turn right and follow the yellow-blazed, narrow swath through the trees. Fields are visible on the left as a side trail comes in from the right. Woodchucks are common in this area; their burrows are just inside the trees at the edge of the field.

After slightly more than one-half mile, the boundary trail angles right and broadens, soon running into the one-lane forest road. Turn left and walk a short distance along the road.

Where the road curves to the right, continue straight on a broad trail blocked by a cable to prevent vehicular access. Continue straight where a side path comes in from the left and then fork right, following the more traveled of two trails. Soon, you will again come onto the one-lane forest road, passing around a cable barricade. To reach the Tyabout Carolina Bay, the largest in the immediate area, turn right on the road and walk about one-tenth mile around the bend. A small area for parking one or two vehicles will come into view on the left. Follow the rough, overgrown trail at the back of this area, descending

132

slightly to the left and arriving at the edge of the depression. The bay covers about one acre, and the water is about four feet deep in the center. Sphagnum moss forms a thick, spongy layer around most of the perimeter. Lichen-encrusted persimmons occur farther in, with dense tangles of buttonbush near the middle. This bay is one of six making up the Blackbird Carolina Bays Nature Preserve.

To continue, make your way back to the forest road and turn right. This route shortly leads to paved Road 471. Cross the road, turn right, walk past a picnic area, and, after slightly less than one-half mile, you will arrive back at the small picnic area where you parked your car.

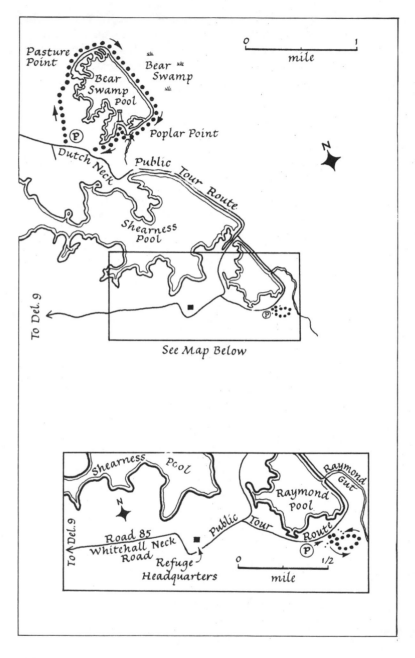

Pasture
Point

Bear
Swamp

Bear
Swamp
Pool

Ⓟ

Poplar Point

Dutch Neck

Public Tour Route

Shearness
Pool

To Del. 9

Ⓟ

0   mile   1

N

See Map Below

Shearness Pool

Raymond Gut

Raymond
Pool

N

Road 85
Whitehall Neck
Road

To Del. 9

Public Tour Route

Ⓟ

Refuge
Headquarters

0   mile   1/2

Bombay Hook National Wildlife Refuge

Two hikes in Delaware's largest expanse of public land

Hiking distance: Raymond Gut, ¼ mile; Bear Swamp Pool, 3 miles
Hiking time: Raymond Gut, ½ hour; Bear Swamp Pool, 1½ hours
Maps: USGS Bombay Hook; refuge map

LOCATED WHERE THE DELAWARE RIVER BROAD-ens into the Delaware Bay, Bombay Hook is the largest single tract of unditched salt, brackish, and freshwater tidal marsh and swamp forest in public ownership in Delaware. This huge expanse of wetlands is immensely important as a fishery and as an outstanding habitat for mammals, waterfowl, shorebirds, wading birds, birds of prey, song birds, reptiles, amphibians, mollusks, crustaceans, and countless other invertebrates. The marshes contribute significantly to the nutrient levels of the Delaware Bay and serve as an important nursery area for blue crab, weakfish (the state fish of Delaware), flounder, black sea bass, striped bass, white perch, eels, spot, and northern diamondback terrapin.

Early Dutch settlers in Delaware called this region "Boompies Hoock." They trapped muskrats and diamondback terrapins, fished the tidal streams, hunted waterfowl, and cut salt marsh hay from the large expanses of wetlands. Today the area is called Bombay Hook and is the largest National Wildlife Refuge on the Delmarva Peninsula. Its 16,280 acres consist mostly of low-lying, marshy islands situated along the edge of the Delaware Bay, with more extensive marshes landward of the islands. The average elevation of the refuge is approximately ten feet. Only about one thousand acres of land are high enough to escape tidal influences. These uplands are wooded or grass covered.

Bombay Hook is intensively managed to develop and protect desirable habitat for migratory birds. For example, many fields have been planted with fescue and other grasses to provide supplemental food supplies for waterfowl. As a result of this management, excellent opportunities exist for nature study. Endangered birds of prey, such as the bald eagle, osprey, and peregrine falcon, nest on or use the refuge. Tremendous numbers of waterfowl arrive each autumn either to spend the winter or to rest during their southward migration. Estimates place the waterfowl population during peak periods at over 115,000 individuals, of which about 100,000 are geese. The marshes harbor the majority of Delaware's snow goose population (an estimated 30,000 birds) during the winter. Leaflets, available from the refuge office, list 261 species of birds and 33 species of mammals. Bombay Hook is one of the best places in Delaware to see white-tailed deer.

Most of the refuge is remote and inaccessible to foot travelers. The two hikes described here only brush the edge of one of nature's most spectacular exhibitions — the tidal marsh. By walking, you may gain an appreciation of the immense grandeur of a coastal marsh in one of this country's finest natural areas. Mosquitoes and other biting insects can make this walk almost unbearable in the warmer months. Either come equipped with repellent or schedule your visit during cooler periods.

The first walk leads to Raymond Gut, one of the myriad intersecting tidal streams that lace the great marshes. This easy, figure-eight path is excellent for families with young children. The trail passes through a small wooded area, skirts brackish pools, and then goes over the tidal marsh on a long boardwalk to the edge of Raymond Gut. Though only one-quarter mile long, this path will enable you to observe plants adapted to a salty environment and to see some of the animals that make the tidal marsh their home.

Our second walk begins on Dutch Neck and proceeds north through grasslands and woods on a spit of fast land known as Pasture Point. You then follow the dike that separates the impounded Bear Swamp Pool on the right from Bear Swamp on the left. The pool is a freshwater impoundment designed to produce aquatic food plants for waterfowl. Bear Swamp is a brackish wetland. You then turn back toward Dutch

136

Neck along another peninsula named Poplar Point. Except for a short spur to an observation tower, this three-mile circuit hike follows an unpaved road that serves as a side loop for the refuge's public tour route; therefore, you may encounter vehicles on the walk. I have not, however, found this part of the refuge heavily visited during most seasons.

ACCESS

Bombay Hook National Wildlife Refuge is near Smyrna and approximately ten miles northeast of Dover. From Dover, go east on DE 8 for 3.5 miles. Turn left (north) and travel 7.6 miles on DE 9. Turn right (east) on Road 85 (Whitehall Neck Road) and drive 2.2 miles to the end of the pavement and the entrance to the refuge. The refuge office, immediately on the left, provides public restrooms and leaflets including maps and lists of animals. When inside the refuge, follow the unpaved, one-way automobile tour route 0.8 mile to a sign on the right that reads "Trail." To take the one-quarter-mile Raymond Gut trail, park your car here on the grassy shoulder. To reach the Bear Swamp Pool trail, continue to follow the one-way tour route around Raymond Pool for 0.9 mile to a "T" junction. Turn right, following the road around Shearness Pool. After 1.5 miles, a one-way road turns off to the right; this road will be your return trail while walking. Drive another 0.3 mile to the next intersection and park your car on the shoulder.

TRAIL:
Raymond Gut

The trail is roughly in the form of a figure eight. Enter the woods on a wood-chip path. A small pool is visible on the left and another one soon comes into view on the right. Fork right, and then stay left where a short spur angles right to the water's edge.

You soon come to the middle of the eight — a wooden bridge across a small channel. Cross the bridge and continue on the wood-chip trail, turning right at the fork. You will shortly leave the woods and start across the tidal marsh on a wide boardwalk. The great sweep of the marsh is before you, the horizon broken only by a stand of distant trees growing on a bit of fast land called Georges Island.

Continue on the boardwalk to the edge of Raymond Gut. A *gut* is

137

a small and serpentine saltwater appendage to a larger tidal creek or river. Depending on the time of day, you may find Raymond Gut still and full of water or you may discover expanses of mud flats exposed to the ceaseless searchings of shorebirds. At other times, the water may be seen surging back or forth through the gut, following the pull and tug of the moon.

Circle back toward the woods, coming again onto a wood-chip path. A side spur to the right leads to a wood duck nesting box and the edge of the pool. Continue toward the left and you will shortly return to the center of the figure eight. Once across the bridge, fork right, following the trail out of the woods and back to your car.

TRAIL:
Bear Swamp Pool

Walk north on the dirt road to begin your clockwise circuit around Bear Swamp Pool. Vehicles drive this segment in a counterclockwise direction, so you will always face approaching traffic during your hike.

The road initially crosses grassland but eventually enters an upland forest. As the road angles to the northeast, you soon leave the trees behind. Bear Swamp Pool appears on the right and Bear Swamp, an expanse of tideland that stretches 2½ miles to the open waters of the Delaware Bay, sweeps away on the left.

The road circles the pool and eventually turns southwest. Just beyond a bridge, at about two miles into the hike, a parking lot will appear on the right with a trail leading one-tenth mile through trees to an observation tower overlooking the pool. Climb the tower for a bird's-eye view of the wetlands.

After descending, turn right at the foot of the tower and follow a circuitous path back to the parking lot. Here, turn right and walk one-third mile to the main public tour route. Turn right again and proceed the final one-third mile to your waiting car.

Norman G. Wilder Wildlife Area

An upland forest walk featuring mistletoe, holly, and clubmoss

Hiking distance: 10 miles
Hiking time: 5 hours
Maps: USGS Marydel and
  Wyoming; wildlife area map

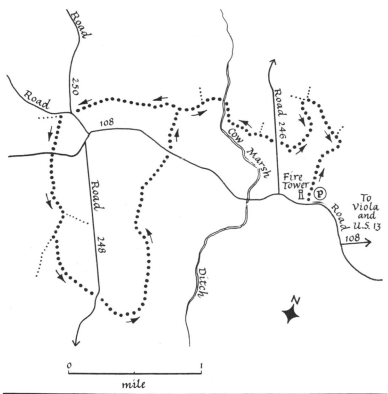

A NARROW, NORTH–SOUTH SPINE OF UPLAND

splits the Coastal Plain in central and southern Delaware. Although hardly classifiable as highland — the terrain is generally flat and rarely exceeds sixty feet in elevation — the height is sufficient to divide the watersheds of the Chesapeake and Delaware bays. This hike traverses one area of this subdivide, a land of tall trees, dense undergrowth, and upland swamp. The water and vegetation make much of the land virtually impenetrable to the average hiker, but you can explore both the forest and the swamp with relative ease from logging and fire roads. Most of your hike will be on the Chesapeake side of the subdivide, but you will begin and end in the Delaware Bay watershed. The subdivide is not well defined due to poor drainage and almost uniform elevation.

The state wildlife area lying athwart the subdivide is named in honor of noted biologist and conservationist Norman G. Wilder. A native of Massachusetts, Wilder worked as a wildlife biologist in New England before being named director of the Delaware Game and Fish Commission (at the time, the agency responsible for managing the state's wildlife areas) in 1948. When Delaware's Department of Natural Resources and Environmental Control was established in 1970, Wilder became the assistant to the secretary. Although presently out of government service, Wilder remains active in many outdoor and conservation organizations.

Some old maps and a few old-time residents still refer to this area by its former name — Petersburg Wildlife Area. I have also seen it shown erroneously on some maps as the Norman G. Wilder Conservation Area. Hunting is a main activity in this and other wildlife areas in Delaware; if you must hike during hunting season, take proper precautions such as wearing bright clothing. Mosquitoes are numerous, so repellent is advisable.

ACCESS

From Dover, go south on U.S. 13 for 8.3 miles to the village of Canterbury. Turn right onto Road 32 and drive 0.7 mile to the intersection with Roads 108 and 240 in the hamlet of Viola. Go straight across the intersection onto Road 108, cross the railroad tracks, and drive 1.1 miles to a stop sign. Turn right and continue on Road 108 for 0.5 mile to the Norman G. Wilder Wildlife Area headquarters

140

building and workshop on the right. Park in the vicinity of the bulletin board, out of the way of maintenance and service vehicles.

TRAIL

From the parking area, walk north (away from Road 108) on a dirt lane. The wildlife area's workshop is on the right and a fire lookout tower is visible above the trees on your left. The lane, a part of the fire road network within the wildlife area, initially crosses fields then angles right into the woods. The forest here is fairly young with a comparatively open canopy. Predominant trees include loblolly pine, tulip tree, hackberry, and sweetgum. The understory is characterized by black bayberry, highbush blueberry, and American holly.

At about 1¼ miles into the hike look for clubmoss growing on the forest floor. This stand of clubmoss extends, off and on, along both sides of the trail for about the next three-fourths mile. Sometimes known as lycopodium, ground pine, running pine, or ground cedar, these plants have become less common in parts of their ranges due to overharvesting for Christmas foliage displays and other decorative purposes. Standing ten to twelve inches tall with soft, luxuriant, evergreen leaves, the plants resemble miniature conifers, often with tiny, cylindrical "cones" at the tips. They create one of the most delicate and delightful sights in the eastern forests.

The pathway skirts a brushy field (a former timbered area) on the right. Just beyond, the fire road turns sharply to the left. Soon after this turn you will see another fire road going off to the right. Keep straight. Eventually, another fire road blocked by vertical wood poles goes to the right, and another ill-defined trail goes straight. Turn left here, keeping on the wide, well-maintained fire road. A ditch and earth barricade have been placed across the fire road where it comes out on paved Road 246. Scramble over or around the obstacles, cross Road 246, and continue east on the fire road (here used occasionally by vehicles).

The fire road soon enters a magnificent stand of white, chestnut, and willow oaks. Mature trees on either side of the trail exceed a hundred feet in height and thirty inches in diameter. Large red maples, scrub pines, and American hollies are also scattered throughout this section. American mistletoe growing in the high branches of the tall trees can be seen along the trail during the leafless seasons. Mistletoe

141

is a parasitic plant and obtains all its nourishment by tapping the host tree's tissues. Shrubs and small trees, such as sweetgum, sweetbay magnolia, swamp azalea, highbush blueberry, deerberry, southern arrowwood, red cedar, strawberry-bush, common greenbrier, and Japanese honeysuckle, round out the woody plants the hiker can observe.

Pass a fire road on the right and a parking area among tall pines on the left. At 2½ miles, the trail crosses Cow Marsh Ditch, a man-made channel designed to draw off water. The soils in this section are very poorly drained, characteristic of upland flats and depressions in this part of the country, and have a black surface layer high in organic matter. The water in Cow Marsh Ditch is stained brown to black due to the heavy organic load.

A fire road will appear on the right and, at three miles, another fire road comes in from the left through a recently logged area. This latter fire road is used for your return loop, but for now keep straight, paralleling the northern boundary of the wildlife area for the next three-fourths mile.

Our walk comes out upon paved Road 108 where it intersects with gravel Road 250. Go straight (west) on Road 108 for one-tenth mile, then turn left (south) into the woods on another fire road. A branching fire road, barricaded by bulldozed earth, turns off immediately to the right. Keep straight and continue south on the fire road, crossing a dirt road at 4¾ miles into the hike and subsequently passing a small parking area and a barricaded fire road on the left. Our main fire road angles right here. Stay on it for another one-tenth mile and then turn left (east) onto another fire road, scrambling around or over an earthen blockade.

The forest in this southern section is drier because the soil is a well-drained, deep loam instead of the sandy loams found more generally in the northern stretches. For about one-half mile the trail leads through a mature oak forest with American holly forming most of the understory.

Another earthen barricade must be traversed just before you come upon paved Road 248. Cross the road and continue on the fire road. Just as the path enters the woods, make your way around another bulldozed blockade. The fire road then angles to the left (north) in a recently timbered area. Wildlife managers have set aside the woods left of the pathway as a game refuge. The area on the right however is open to hunting during season. Some logging activity has occurred recently in small tracts.

Walk 1¾ miles, cross paved Road 108, go around a high earthen barricade, and continue north on the fire road. In one-quarter mile, you will come upon a recently logged area on your left and shortly thereafter a "T" junction with the fire road on which you started this hike. Turn right and retrace your steps three miles to the parking lot.

Killens Pond State Park

Around an old millpond on the Murderkill River

Hiking distance: 2½ miles
Hiking time: 1½ hours
Maps: USGS Harrington; park map

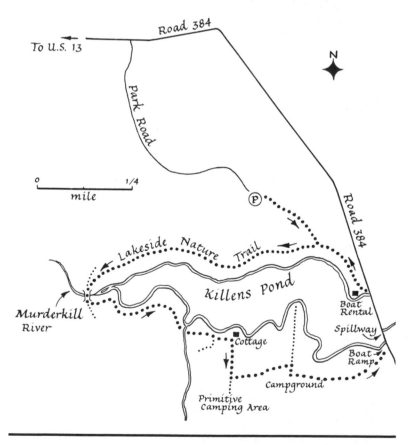

KILLENS POND PRESENTS A STUDY IN CONTRASTS. It lies in the midst of rich farmland and, as such, shares the fate of most bodies of water facing agricultural runoff. Erosion from farmland not only clogs the watershed streams that feed Killens, but also fills the pond with sediment, increases turbidity, and contributes to pollution from pesticides, fertilizers, and animal wastes that permeate the silt load. Of all these assaults, excessive nitrate pollution from fertilizers and animal wastes is probably of chief concern because of its potential hazard to human health. Due to persistently high nitrate levels in Killens Pond, the state of Delaware closed the public beach and built a concrete pool with chlorinated water for swimmers.

On the bright side, the pond still serves as a focal point for recreation and for the plants and animals that depend upon it for sustenance, shelter, and breeding habitats. Fishermen prize the largemouth bass, pickeral, crappie, and bluegill they pull from Killens. River otters hunt and play in its waters. Raccoons search the shoreline and the shallows for food and raise their young in the hollow trees of the surrounding forest. Ring-billed gulls usually can be seen soaring over the open water. In the winter, large numbers of whistling swans use the pond as an overnight resting place. A true sense of wildness can be experienced by standing on the shore on a February evening and watching these great white birds, with wingspreads up to seven feet, descend from the sky. Occasional pairs arrive at first, followed by small groups of six to eight birds, then larger flocks of fifteen to twenty. Each arrival is occasion for high-pitched, amiable chattering among all the swans. Soon the darkening waters are filled with a resonant uproar that reverberates from shore to shore. The spectacle is repeated at daybreak. A few birds take flight at first light while others leave later in larger groups. Once airborne, these flocks usually circle the pond to gain altitude and to get into flying formation, cooing all the while, before heading out to feed in the fields and marshes.

The plant community surrounding the pond will also delight the hiker at any season. Most noticeable are the tall trees, especially the tulip trees, oaks, and loblolly pines. A few of the park's latter species are infested with fungi or viruses that cause the needles to grow in thick, tufted clumps on some of the high branches. Such irregularities are called witches'-brooms due to their fanciful similarities to sinister supernatural objects.

In late winter and early spring, the low-lying areas along the trail brighten with the large, green leaves of skunk cabbage. Later in the

145

year, ladyslippers grace the forest floor and dogwoods add splashes of white to the understory.

Killens was originally a millpond made by damming the Murderkill River. Evidence of the old grist mill no longer exists and today the sixty-six-acre pond is a natural area in central Delaware. The trail featured in this hike (totaling 2½ miles) circles the pond, mostly through a mixed deciduous-coniferous forest. A one-tenth-mile segment is along a paved road.

ACCESS

Killens Pond State Park is located near Felton. To reach our trailhead, go south from Dover on U.S. 13 for 10.8 miles. Turn left onto Road 384 and travel 1.2 miles to the park entrance on the right. Go 0.7 mile to the end of the park road and leave your car in the large parking lot.

TRAIL

From the parking lot, walk southeast on the unpaved maintenance road, winding through the pine-shaded picnic area and following signs that read "Watercraft Rental". As you top a small rise, Killens Pond comes into view. Turn right onto the Lakeside Nature Trail and start your hike around the pond.

The Lakeside Trail has numbered posts that correspond to numbered entries in a trail leaflet available from park rangers. The path skirts beautiful stands of American holly (the state tree of Delaware) that grow profusely along the swampy margins of the pond. Giant loblolly pines and tulip trees are found on drier ground overlooking the water. Just beyond post 13, you cross a low area on a wooden bridge with the inscription "YCC 76" carved into the plank deck. The YCC (Youth Conservation Corps) made most of the trail improvements you are using on today's hike.

The pathway eventually crosses an abandoned township road. Turn left, toward the pond, and cross the slow-flowing Murderkill River on a long, wooden bridge (another YCC project). Once on the bridge, you leave the Lakeside Nature Trail (which retraces its steps along the old township road and stays on the north shore of the pond) and enter a less-developed portion of the park. Here at the upper reaches of the pond is an ideal place to stop for a few minutes and catch sight of some of the birds inhabiting this area. A belted kingfisher may come

146

rattling by, or you may spot a great blue heron stalking fish in the shallows. Song sparrows are common in the shrubs that line the banks and barred owls frequent the tall trees at twilight.

When across the bridge, turn left immediately (leaving the old road) and follow the trail along the shoreline. Cross a short, wooden bridge over a sluggish inlet and turn left again. The trail continues to skirt the shore, crossing inlets and swampy areas on bridges. After ascending a small knoll, the trail forks. The right forks leads away from the pond and circles back to the old township road. Take the left fork (the straighter choice) and stay parallel to the shoreline.

Eventually you will come upon a white frame cottage on a knoll overlooking the pond. Stay behind the cottage and turn right (away from the water) on a dirt road. The park's primitive youth camping area is visible in a large grassy area ahead of you. Walk toward the primitive camping area, then turn left into the woods just before the road enters the grassy expanse. There is no obvious trail through the woods, but the forest floor is open and walking is easy. In the winter, watch for tiny bands of chickadees or titmice darting from tree to tree.

Leave the youth camping area behind and immediately enter the park's family campground. Skirt the campsites, staying between the campground and the shore. A woodland path soon forms; follow it until it comes to a "T" at a wide trail. A short spur to the left takes you to a high, wooded promontory that juts out into the pond — a good place to enjoy sunrises and sunsets. To continue the circuit hike, turn right and follow the broad trail toward one of the campground loop roads. Just before reaching the campsites, turn left off the trail and make your way through the forest. Once again the way is clear and a trailway soon develops parallel to the shoreline.

Continue around the pond, crossing a small, wet area on sawed logs and arriving in the dirt parking lot for the boat launching ramp. Cross the lot and turn left on paved Road 384 which crosses the dam impounding Killens Pond.

When over the dam turn left off the road, go around a chain-link fence, and then cross the lawn surrounding the watercraft rental concession stands. Turn right onto the dirt maintenance road. This road leads shortly to the Lakeside Nature Trail entrance on the left and then to the lot where you parked your vehicle.

Prime Hook National Wildlife Refuge

History and wildlife in the marshes bordering Delaware Bay

Hiking distance: 1¼ miles
Hiking time: ¾ hour
Maps: USGS Lewes and Milton

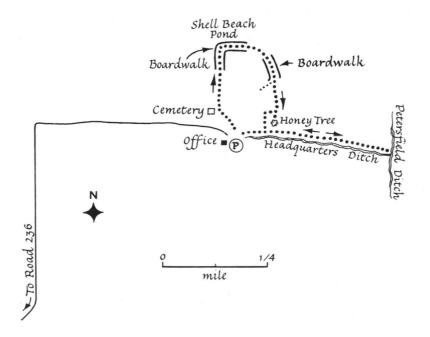

THIS HIKE FEATURES A LOT OF VARIETY IN A SHORT distance. Beginning in upland fields bordered by wild roses and pocketed with woodchuck burrows, the trail goes by a nineteenth-century cemetery before reaching a boardwalk into a marsh. The path then loops back through a wooded swamp, passing a gnarled tree housing a colony of honeybees. Next, a spur takes you down a service road beside a narrow waterway opening into an expansive marsh, a great sea of reeds and grasses dotted with a few forested hummocks.

Prime Hook is the smaller of the two national wildlife refuges in Delaware. Excellent opportunities exist at any season for observing birds, mammals, and other wildlife. Spring and autumn are especially good times to view waterfowl because Prime Hook is primarily a migratory refuge. During these seasons, tens of thousands of birds use the refuge as a resting and feeding area during their migrations along the Atlantic flyway. The normally quiet ponds and creeks become crowded with noisy concentrations of ducks and geese. Peak periods vary depending on the weather, but generally the few days around March 15 and November 1 are best for witnessing this age-old pageant-in-the-sky.

In addition to today's walk, the short Pine Grove Trail and a few service roads provide other opportunities for hiking at Prime Hook. Dogs are permitted when leashed. Part of our trail was built by the Youth Conservation Corps.

ACCESS

From Georgetown, drive east on U.S. 9 for 5.8 miles. Turn left (north) on DE 5, driving 5.0 miles to Milton. There turn right (east) on DE 16 and go 3.8 miles to Road 236. Turn left and enter the refuge in only 0.1 mile. Continue on the refuge road for 1.4 miles until it dead-ends into the parking lot at the refuge office.

TRAIL

On the north side of the parking area, follow a sign that says "Boardwalk" along a broad trail bordered by hedgerows of multiflora rose. Another sign farther along cautions you to avoid stepping in any of the numerous woodchuck burrows lying hidden in the tall grass.

The way soon passes by the old Morris family burying ground on the left. The Morris estate once stood near this spot but was torn down around 1968. The cemetery, riddled with woodchuck dens and partly

149

shaded by ragged black walnuts, is remarkably well preserved, thanks to the protection it receives from the federal government. Most burials date from the mid-1800s. The inscription on one weathered grey stone, barely decipherable after all these years, offers some grim advice to hikers and others who walk this way:

> Behold ye stranger that pass by
> As you are now so once was I
> As I am now so must you be
> Prepare for death and follow me.

Beyond the graveyard, the trail leaves fast land and goes out upon the edges of Shell Beach Pond by means of a boardwalk. Fine views of the marsh that covers most of the refuge can be enjoyed from the boardwalk.

You soon loop back to solid ground and pass through a small forested area. This area becomes a wooded swamp, and another boardwalk keeps the trail above water. Turn left off the boardwalk (just before it enters a field) and walk along an earthen berm that continues to skirt the swamp. Where the trail turns sharply right, a very short spur leads straight to an overlook at the base of an old tree used by honeybees. Their entrance is through the hollow end of a high, broken branch.

To continue, return to the main trail, which leads immediately across a small ditch into an open field. Turn left and head for an opening through a hedgerow. The break leads to a service road that parallels Headquarters Ditch, a man-made channel allowing boat access from the refuge office to the creeks and rivers that course through the marsh. Turn left and follow the service road. A few forested clumps along the trail and in the midst of the marsh represent the small, sandy hummocks, a few feet higher than the rest of the terrain and consequently drier. Many of the little islands of trees are known to have served as temporary camps for Indians who came to the marsh to fish, hunt, and gather shellfish and crabs.

Bird life is abundant due to the varied habitat. The tree-covered hummocks provide shelter for many birds not normally encountered in marshland. Owls roost in the branches, using the woody islands as a base for their nighttime forays. Flickers, red-bellied woodpeckers, mockingbirds, and warblers fly about. Out on the open marsh, you will likely see red-winged blackbirds flitting along the ditch, vultures circling overhead, gulls soaring by, and perhaps a northern harrier

150

sailing low over the tall reeds in its unmistakable, buoyant hunting flight. Waterfowl abounds during migrations.

Walk about 0.4 mile to the end of the service road where Headquarters Ditch comes upon Petersfield Ditch in a "T" intersection. Turn around and hike straight back the service road to the parking area.

Cape Henlopen
State Park

*A varied circuit hike featuring
bay shore, ocean beach, sand
dunes, forest, bogs, and salt
marsh*

Hiking distance: 7 miles
Hiking time: 3½ hours
Maps: USGS Cape Henlopen;
  park map

CAPE HENLOPEN WAS IDENTIFIED ON SPANISH maps of the New World as early as 1544. The English navigator Henry Hudson, sailing under the Dutch flag in 1609, found a snug haven behind the cape for his ship the *Half Moon* and claimed the area for Holland. Dutch settlers arrived in 1631, but the colony was annihilated by Indians. A second colonization, in 1658, was successful.

The cape is one of present-day Delaware's most prominent landmarks, a dynamic peninsula jutting boldly from the land. The Atlantic surf pounds the eastern shore. Waves and wind constantly chisel and hew the shoreline into new shapes and forms, inexorably resculpting the cape's profile. On the west, by contrast, lies a quiet harbor where gentle waves allow the sand to settle and accumulate and thus add to the measure of the land.

Since Cape Henlopen is a landscape in flux, it is often exquisitely beautiful and always endlessly fascinating. In spite of the harsh and rapidly changing environment, the plant and animal communities of the shore are fragile and remarkably diverse. The beach itself is home to an array of living things, usually augmented by whatever the sea casts up. The dunes, the most unstable of the cape's environments, nevertheless are often covered with beach grass, beach heather, broomsedge, and switchgrass. The more stable parts of the cape support mature forests of pine, oak, cherry, cedar, and a host of smaller associated shrubs such as highbush blueberry and sassafras. Interspersed in the woodlands are small bogs rich in cranberries and sundews. The salt marshes behind the dunes and the forests are densely covered with salt hay, saltmarsh cordgrass, hightide-bush, and the tall, reedlike phragmites.

White-tailed deer are common in the woodlands. Bobwhites abound both on the dunes and in the forests; in summer opportunities prevail to see family broods — mother, father, and their host of chicks. Seabirds and shorebirds are abundant. Mosquitoes and deer flies are common, too, especially off the beach, so repellent is suggested for this walk.

Cape Henlopen is the site of a former military installation, one of the key posts in this country's coastal defense network during World War II. Today most of the military lands have been turned into a state park — Delaware's largest — but the army and navy still retain control over small parcels. Some old unexploded ammunition may yet occur on the military lands. For this reason, and because of the dense stands of poison ivy, it is advisable to stay on the trail.

The walk recommended here follows parts of both nature trails in the park. Hikes along the entire lengths of these trails provide additional walks that are enjoyable and educational. Brochures describing the trails are available from rangers or from the Seaside Nature Center. Please read the section on beach walking in the Introduction of this book before hiking the cape.

ACCESS

From Georgetown, go east on U.S. 9 for 17.0 miles to Cape Henlopen State Park. Once inside the park, continue straight for 0.3 mile to the Seaside Nature Center on the left. Park your car in the center's lot.

TRAIL

Walk around to the left of the nature center and begin your hike on the Seaside Nature Trail. Numbered stations are keyed to the descriptive leaflet explaining items of interest along the path. The trail winds through the low dunes. Black rat snakes frequent the thickets, foraging for lizards, toads, and small birds and mammals. Their sinuous tracks can often be seen along open, sandy stretches of the path.

After about one-fourth mile, the trail comes out onto the beach of Breakwater Harbor, a broad cove of the Delaware Bay. A long fishing pier is to the left and a lighthouse stands on the stone breakwater that guards the harbor. Turn right and walk along the beach.

The bay shore is almost always a scene of activity. Shorebirds, terns, and gulls search the beach and the shallow water for food. Various forms of marine life have been cast onto the beach: oysters, mussels, slipper shells, razor clams, and horseshoe crabs are abundant. Delaware Bay is renowned for its large populations of horseshoe crabs. At times, it is almost impossible to walk this trail without stepping on them or their skeletons. Tens of thousands of horseshoe crabs come shoreward during high spring tides to mate in the shallows and to lay their eggs on the beach. Thousands die when they become stranded, their skeletons forming a low, ragged wall at the high tide mark.

The Seaside Nature Trail soon turns right and reenters the dunes. Continue straight, along the shore. The Maritime Exchange Tower will appear on the right. Observers in the tower dispatch navigational pilots to incoming vessels and also notify port operators up the bay of ship arrivals.

After the tower, the shore begins angling northward toward the tip of Cape Henlopen. Follow the shoreline, noting the long tongues of

154

sand and mud that extend into the harbor. These accreted spits of land, best seen at low tide, have been formed by sediments carried by the erosional forces of wind and water from the seaward side of the cape. They are present-day evidence of the erosion and migration of the cape that has been occurring for at least the last 11,000 years. Geologists describe the spread of the sea over land areas and the consequent sedimentation on older deposits as transgression. Additional transgression will eventually enable these spits to gain height and length and be transformed into dunes far removed from the migrating shoreline. Later, our trail crosses some larger, ancient recurved spit tips that had their origin as small sand bars on the bay side of old Cape Henlopen. They are now thickly forested and are located about 1½ miles inland to the south.

The rolling dunes on the right, lying in the heart of the peninsula, serve as an important seabird colony. Piping plovers, black skimmers, and least and common terns nest here. No entry is permitted into this area during nesting season. By staying close to the shore, and by preventing your dog from wandering into the dunes, you can help assure the successful rearing of the next generation of these birds.

At the tip of Cape Henlopen, where the land, bay, and ocean meet, you will come out onto a very broad expanse of open beach, broken only occasionally by small, isolated clumps of vegetation. A lighthouse sits on a breakwater off the coast and guides mariners to safety with both a beacon and a horn. Fully automated, it replaced the original Cape Henlopen lighthouse erected in 1725. The old lighthouse, built on land and victim of the eroding shoreline, fell to the sea in 1926.

Curve to the right, turning south in a gradual arc, and walk along the ocean beach. After almost one mile, you will enter a surf fishing area, with dune crossings for both foot travelers and off-road vehicles. Continue south for about another mile to the life-guarded swimming area. Turn right, off the beach, on the first walkway over the dunes and then turn left, walking through the parking lot behind the bathhouse. Water, food, and telephone are available here in season. Beyond the bathhouse, at the edge of the parking area, angle left on a dirt road that stays behind the primary dune. Stunted pitch pines grow on the back dunes and, along with other plants, help anchor the sand with their roots. After about one-fourth mile, a crossroad intersects the trail. The land ahead is Fort Miles, an army installation, and entry here is prohibited. Turn left (east), cross the primary dune, and then turn right (south) along the ocean beach.

The long beaches of Cape Henlopen provide opportunities for solitude and escape.

The trail soon enters Fort Miles. Stay along the ocean in this area to insure passage. The headland to the west overlooking the sea is Sand Hill, also known as the Great Dune. Stretching to about ninety feet above sea level, it is the highest point along the Atlantic between

156

Massachusetts and North Carolina. Military strategists recognized the importance of this high land near the mouth of Delaware Bay and built a fort there. The old concrete bunkers, part of the coastal defenses during World War II, still stand on Sand Hill and at other nearby places. Like nearly everything else at Cape Henlopen, Sand Hill is not static; it is slowly migrating south.

As you continue south, you will come upon a dune-crossing road marking your reentry into the state park; go straight, staying on the beach. Battery Smith and Battery Herring (built in 1941 and 1942 respectively), former navy gun emplacements, can be seen on the high dunes. Part of this area remains a naval reserve facility. A few weathered tree stumps awash in the surf attest to the slow, westward erosion of the beach. Pass a long groin of stone boulders, a beach stabilization technique, jutting into the sea. South of the groin, a pedestrian gate is in the broken fence that formerly enclosed the old navy base. Climb the dune to the gate and make your way through or around it. Take the path to a paved road and follow it around the back of Battery Herring.

Opposite a paved road on the right that leads up to Battery Herring, turn left onto a lane largely overgrown with bush-clovers and other plants. A log bearing a "No Vehicles" sign stretches across the entrance to the lane. The herbaceous vegetation clears as the lane descends slightly and enters a forested region known as the Flat Sands. Bracken forms dense stands in places while loblolly pine is the predominant tree.

About one-half mile from the paved road, you will come upon a broad cross trail (an old military road) — turn right (northwest). Side trails will be encountered, but continue straight for almost a mile as the old road crosses low, sandy, densely forested ridges, alternated with marshland. These ridges are the recurved spit tips mentioned earlier. They are the relics of old Cape Henlopen, deposits of sand and gravel formerly near the cape's tip and left behind in ancient times by wind and waves. The marshes represent remnants of a shallow lagoon, much like today's Breakwater Harbor, that remained unsilted during the cape evolution. Our trail bisects the narrow tongues of sandy ridge and salt marsh which resemble the interlocking fingers of folded hands upon the landscape. Old shells have been used to raise the road surface above the waters of the marsh.

The road becomes paved with asphalt as it passes a cinder block building on the right. Continue straight on the pavement, passing a fenced enclosure on the right containing atmospheric monitoring equip-

157

ment, and coming upon a gate in a high fence. The gate is chained but not locked. Pass through the gate (being sure to rechain it securely) and turn right on a paved road. (If you cannot get through the gate, simply turn right and walk along the fence which ends in about two hundred feet, allowing you to walk on the road.) An old ammunition storage bunker, mostly buried in the hillside, is seen at the road junction.

The road climbs very gradually; in just a short distance, turn left at the first opportunity onto a paved road that angles in from the left rear. This old road continues uphill and passes another ammunition bunker and the park's campground on the right. The gradual climb ends at a steel cable drawn across the road, where our trail enters the main campground road. This is the crest of the back slope of Sand Hill, with an elevation of about forty feet. The tall, silolike tower visible on the left is one of a series of similar structures used by the military during World War II as an observation post to spot enemy vessels on the ocean and to direct the fire of the shore batteries. Fine views of Delaware Bay are afforded to the north. Continue straight, descending slightly on the boulevard-like campground road, past the campground entrance station, a paved parking lot, and the trailer sewage dumping station.

Turn right where the road forks and then bear right onto a concrete road. Cross the road diagonally and bear left off the road just beyond the "Speed Limit 25" sign. In a few steps you will intersect the Pinelands Nature Trail in the vicinity of station number 15. Turn right and continue through the numbered stations (16, 17, 18, etc.), keyed to the leaflet that describes the natural and human history of the pinelands.

Follow the nature trail for slightly over one mile, coming out of the woods into the old military parade ground. Cross the open field and the road to the Seaside Nature Center.

Delaware Seashore State Park

A walk along the Atlantic Ocean

Hiking distance: 6¼ miles
Hiking time: 3 hours
Maps: USGS Bethany Beach and
  Rehoboth Beach; park map

IN MY OPINION, THE STATE OF DELAWARE SHOULD be commended for its farsighted and aggressive beach conservation policies. Though with only about twenty-six miles of Atlantic coastline (the least of any eastern seaboard state except New Hampshire), Delaware has set aside three state parks totaling more than five thousand acres, protecting about fifteen miles (approximately 58 percent) of the state's shoreline. Neighboring states have lagged behind. Maryland, with slightly more oceanfront than the First State, has established only one small state park protecting two miles of shore. Virginia, which has well over one hundred miles of shoreline, is developing its first ocean park in a secluded section of Virginia Beach; no state parks exist on the Virginia Eastern Shore. New Jersey, with about five times as much oceanfront as Delaware, has only four state parks on the shore protecting about 3,600 acres. Fortunately, federal preserves (such as national seashores and national wildlife refuges) and private lands owned by conservation groups help preserve the wild character of some of the shore in these states.

The Delaware ocean parks are not pristine — off-road vehicles have access to most of the beach and a four-lane highway runs just behind the front dune along much of the coast — but they are semi-wild. Those who do not mind walking can still be alone with the sand and the sea. The dunes are topped with coarse but fragile grass, and shorebirds such as little terns and black skimmers nest on the sands.

159

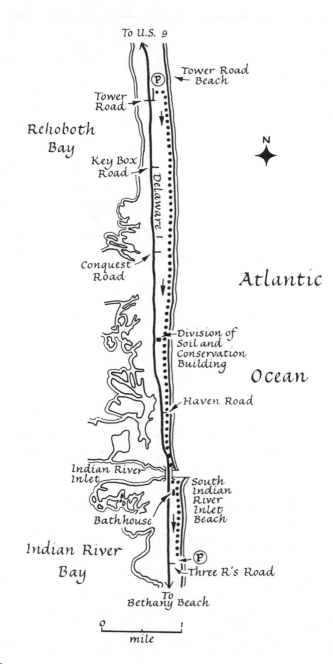

To U.S. 9

Tower Road
Beach

Tower
Road

Rehoboth
Bay

Key Box
Road

Delaware 1

Conquest
Road

N

Atlantic

Division of
Soil and
Conservation
Building

Ocean

Haven Road

Indian River
Inlet

South
Indian
River
Inlet
Beach

Bathhouse

Indian River
Bay

Three R's Road

To
Bethany Beach

0   1
mile

The marshes on the bayside teem with wildlife; Rehoboth and Indian River bays have the greatest concentration of nesting ospreys in the state. If you hike along the beach in June, you will likely sight adult male ospreys flying out to sea and returning with large fish grasped in their talons, bound for their nests and their ravenous young.

Delaware Seashore State Park occupies a narrow sand reef separating the Atlantic from Rehoboth and Indian River bays. The park has no designated hiking trails. The walk recommended here simply follows the beach. This hike is best done with two cars; if you cannot arrange this convenience, you will have to return by the same route, thus doubling your mileage. Be sure to read the section on beach walking in the Introduction before attempting this hike.

ACCESS

From Georgetown, drive east on U.S. 9 for 11.9 miles to the junction with DE 1. Turn right (south) on DE 1, enter Delaware Seashore State Park after 7.5 miles, and continue through the park for 5.9 miles to Three R's Road. Turn left and leave one car in the gravel parking lot. Then return north on DE 1 for 5.6 miles, turn right onto Tower (or Towers) Road, and leave the second car in the large, paved lot.

TRAIL

From the parking lot, cross the sand dunes on the southernmost walkway to Tower Road Beach, a lifeguarded area during the swimming season. Turn right (south) and walk along the ocean.

About one-half mile from the swimming beach, a small stand of old tree stumps can be seen protruding above the sand at low tide. Worn smooth by the waves and wind, and covered with rock barnacles and filamentous green algae, their roots continue to hold fast in the soft sand. They are remnants of a so-called "ghost forest" and serve as dramatic examples of the power of the sea. The land along this stretch of shoreline is slowly being eroded westward, the ocean having cut through dunes and shrublands to the onetime tree belt on the bayside. These stumps in time will be reburied by water and sand as the pounding waves wear away portions of the shore.

An area set aside for surf fishing is encountered at about three-fourths mile. Fishermen here and at other places along the oceanfront try for weakfish, striped bass, kingfish, and bluefish. Walkways over the dunes lead to a small, gravel parking lot and Key Box (or Keybox)

161

Road, with access to DE 1. The secluded beaches around Key Box Road and stretching for one mile south to Conquest Road are used by nude bathers, despite occasional discouragement from the Delaware Division of Parks and Recreation.

At 1¾ miles into the hike, you will come upon the Conquest Road surf fishing area, with walkways leading to a small parking lot and DE 1. You will walk along an unfrequented part of the beach for the next 2¾ miles. In one-half mile, a dune crossing for off-road vehicles will appear, followed at one mile by a large, handsome, weathered building behind the dunes. This building is a former Coast Guard station, now serving the Beach Preservation section of the Delaware Division of Soil and Conservation. South of the building, the front or primary dune is very low, in places scarcely higher than the upper beach itself. In this vicinity, the Atlantic has surged across the reef to the bay on an average of once a year during recent years, scouring the land of plants and sand. The area remains sparsely vegetated because of inundations by very high tides during severe storms. Pass the Haven Road surf fishing area and arrive finally at the Indian River Inlet, the only major break along Delaware's entire oceanfront. The area just north of the inlet is set aside as a surfing beach.

Turn away from the ocean at the stone jetty that lines the inlet, walk toward the highway bridge, and climb the steps to the road. Cross the bridge on the sidewalk, but take time to enjoy the spectacular views of the ocean, beach, dunes, and marshes that the high bridge affords. People and birds gather to fish on the jetties that protect the inlet. Common and little terns can be seen from above as they execute breathtaking, headlong dives into the water, often, it appears, dangerously close to the rocks. If successful, they emerge with a small fish in their beaks. Fishermen go after larger species such as flounder, tautog, striped bass, sea bass, weakfish, and bluefish.

The view from the bridge also enables you to observe the effects of man-made jetties on shore erosion. The jetties prevent the channel from filling the sand and so provide fishing boats and pleasure craft access between the Atlantic and Indian River Bay. The result has been a slowly developing but far-reaching change in the character of the beach. Sand has built up along the coast south of the inlet, resulting in a beach extending about nine hundred feet farther into the ocean than the shore north of the inlet. From the bridge you can see that the north beach is undernourished — its sand is still being carried northward by the longshore current but is not being replaced because

162

of the jetties. The great stone walls entirely stop the flowing sand, carrying it into deep water so that even storm waves cannot pick it up and move it along the coast.

Continue across the bridge, descend the steps, and walk toward the ocean. The South Indian River Inlet Beach is a lifeguarded swimming area; public telephones, drinking water, and a snack bar are available in the large bathhouse during season. Continue hiking south along the ocean for about one mile to the surf fishing area at Three R's Road. Cross the dunes on the first designated path to the parking lot.

Fenwick Island State Park

Beach walking in Delaware's
southeastern corner

Hiking distance: 5 miles
Hiking time: 2½ hours
Maps: USGS Assawoman Bay and
  Bethany Beach; park map

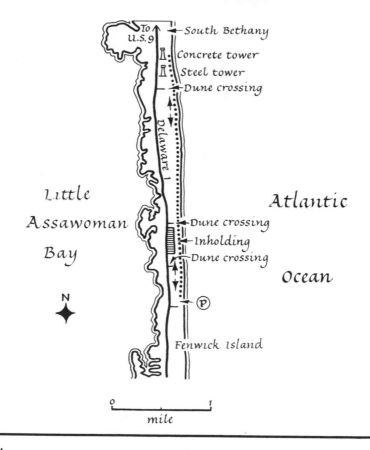

FENWICK ISLAND STATE PARK IS AN OASIS OF OPEN space along the Atlantic Ocean in extreme southeastern Delaware. It is a welcome refuge amid the ocean front developments that stretch nearly fifteen miles from Ocean City, Maryland, to Bethany Beach, Delaware. Here you can experience what Oliver Wendell Holmes in "The Chambered Nautilus" called the "unresting sea." The North Atlantic beats relentlessly, sometimes with short, steep breakers, sometimes sweeping with thunderous rhythm onto the shore with long, widely spaced swells that may have come all the way from Portugal. The park features a wide ocean beach of clean sand and rolling surf backed by a system of low dunes. Various shorebirds, boat-tailed grackles, black skimmers, and several species of gulls and terns frequent the sunstruck beach. I have seen pods of up to twenty dolphins swimming and cavorting in the ocean less than two hundred yards from shore.

Fenwick Island is not an island at all but rather a long, narrow bar extending southward from its connection with the mainland to the Ocean City Inlet in Maryland. It separates the Atlantic from the shallow Assawoman and Little Assawoman bays. A glance at a map shows that this stretch of shore extends farther into the ocean than the rest of the Delmarva coast. If you stand facing seaward on the beach, you might begin to feel as the poet Robinson Jeffers, who wrote in "Continent's End," "I gazing at...the established sea-marks, felt behind me/Mountain and plain, the immense breadth of the continent, before me the mass and doubled stretch of water."

This area was formerly part of Delaware Seashore State Park and is still shown as such on some maps. Read the section on beach walking in the Introduction before your trip. The trail described here begins near the town of Fenwick Island and runs north along the beach for the length of the park, returning the same way. Like any pleasant beach hike, it is ideal for maundering or dawdling; walk as much or as little as you wish.

ACCESS

From Georgetown, drive east on U.S. 9 for 11.9 miles to the junction with DE 1. Turn right (south) on DE 1, enter Fenwick Island State Park after 19.3 miles, and continue through the park for 2.6 miles. Just after you leave the park and enter the town of Fenwick Island, make a U-turn and head north on DE 1. Drive for only about 0.1 mile and then turn right into the beach parking lot.

TRAIL

Go across the primary dune on the northernmost walkway and turn left (north) along the ocean. The beach here is set aside for swimming and surfing.

You soon enter the surf fishing area and, after almost one-half mile, a dune crossing for off-road vehicles is seen. This crossing is followed shortly by a private inholding of beach front condominiums. Residents will likely be crowded onto the beach during pleasant weather; make your way around the beach umbrellas, blankets, and sunbathers and continue northward.

Just beyond the inholding, you will see another off-road vehicle dune crossing, and then you walk along a strand of isolated shore. An occasional beachcomber or fisherman, along with mixed flocks of herring, ring-billed, and great black-backed gulls, may share the solitude.

A third off-road vehicle dune crossing is encountered two miles from the swimming area. About one-fourth mile beyond, an old tower of steel girders stands in the dunes. To complete your hike through the park, continue north another one-fourth mile to a tall, silolike concrete tower just behind the front dune. This tower was one of many built along the Delaware coast during World War II to direct the fire of shore batteries against enemy ships. Today, most have fallen into ruin but a few stand as empty columns, their narrow openings near the top still staring seaward. The houses visible on the dunes to the north, some with their porches extending over the beach, are in South Bethany. Turn and walk back to your car.

Wallops Park

A study in how government decisions affect park land

Hiking distance: 1 mile
Hiking time: ½ hour
Map: USGS Chincoteague West

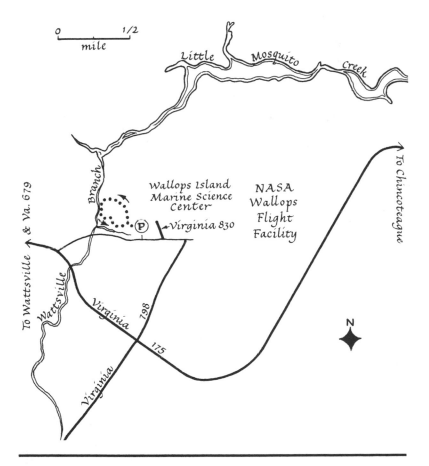

0 ___ 1/2
mile

Little Mosquito Creek

To Chincoteague

Branch

To Wattsville & Va. 679

Wattsville

Wallops Island
Marine Science
Center

NASA
Wallops
Flight
Facility

P

Virginia 830

Virginia 798

Virginia 175

Virginia

N

WALLOPS PARK WAS THE FIRST PARK ESTABLISHED

by the Accomack County Parks and Recreation Commission. It was also the last. In 1977, the federal government gave thirty-two acres of land along Wattsville Branch to Accomack for development as a county park. The property was no longer needed by the nearby Wallops Flight Facility of the National Aeronautics and Space Administration (NASA).

With the land came federal money and assistance. The Young Adult Conservation Corps (YACC) blazed a one-mile, interpretative trail to the creek through a twenty-seven-acre climax forest. The path was developed with numbered stations, a descriptive pamphlet, stairs, a footbridge, benches, an impoundment on a small tributary of Wattsville Branch, wildlife feeding stations, and a special trailside exhibit on soils.

The county turned one of the abandoned government houses (formerly used to quarter NASA employees) into a museum and nature center. People were hired with funds given to the county by the federal government under the Comprehensive Employee Training Act (CETA). The new staff established interpretative programs, built exhibits, and planned nature-related curricula in cooperation with local schools. A five-acre open area on the property was developed into playgrounds, athletic fields, and picnic areas.

Then, federal funds dried up. The YACC was abolished, and the programs established under CETA were canceled. Accomack County let go the recreation workers and closed the museum. Neglect began to take its toll on the park. Some of the picnic grills were vandalized, some of the trail improvements were destroyed and not replaced. The trail right-of-way was no longer maintained.

The athletic fields are still used by Little League baseball and youth football teams; churches hold Sunday afternoon outings in the picnic area. But the grass and brush grow taller each spring and encroach from the perimeter a bit more each year. Few people now walk the forested trail to Wattsville Branch. Wallops Park has an air of interrupted destiny. Tax-poor Accomack County, unable to maintain its single park, has no immediate plans to develop others, a sad comment because preserved places like Wallops Park are important to sustaining a natural balance in our civilized world. Even small parcels of a few acres often enable an ecosystem to remain viable.

Here, the land remains unspoiled and quiet, clothed in tall pines and hardwoods. On the rich forest floor, you can find moccasin flowers, mayapples, jack-in-the-pulpits, cranefly orchids, and at least nine dif-

168

ferent species of ferns. Many hard-pressed animals, once numerous but now experiencing narrowed and polluted habitats, depend on the protective cover provided by the park to raise their young and to supply their food. Part of the Wattsville Branch wetland is preserved, thus enhancing water quality and purity throughout the watershed. Lastly, but just as importantly, human visitors in this setting are able to sample the sights and sounds of wild places.

The trail described here is the old YACC project through the woods. You will be able to assess some of the county's former plans and to inspect the present state of the park as you walk the path. Some downed trees may cause detours, but the way is easy to follow. Mosquitoes are plentiful in season.

ACCESS

From the center of Accomac, go north on U.S. Business 13 for 2.0 miles, continuing north on U.S. 13 for another 2.5 miles to VA 679. Turn right (north) and follow this back road with care where it makes unmarked turns. In 10.2 miles (about 5.4 miles north of Modest Town), keep left at a fork. (Do not become confused by the sign pointing right that says "NASA — Wallops Island".) At a crossroads 1.0 mile north of Atlantic (13.6 miles from U.S. 13), turn left. You will arrive at the junction of VA 175 in Wattsville after 1.4 miles; turn right. Go 1.1 miles and turn left onto VA 798. This road curves sharply to the left after 0.7 mile where a drive to the right enters the main gate of the Wallops Flight Facility. Continue for another 0.3 mile on VA 798, here also marked VA 832. Just after passing VA 830 that leads to the Wallops Island Marine Science Center of the Marine Science Consortium, turn right onto an unpaved lane marked with a sign that reads "Wallops Park and Recreational Area." Leave your car in the dirt parking lot.

TRAIL

The trailhead is in the left corner of the woods as you face west from the parking area, just to the left of a dilapidated, wooden bulletin board covered by a peaked, shingled roof. A box designed to hold trail descriptive pamphlets is now empty.

The path splits just inside the woods, with a leg going off to the right and another, straighter leg descending to a wooden bridge. Turn right here; you will come back to this point along the straight fork.

169

The trail is thickly covered with leaves and pine needles. Just after passing a bench, the way begins to descend, at first slighty and then more steeply down some steps, to the edge of the intertidal Wattsville Branch. A short spur leads right, through the trees to a high fence marking NASA property.

Turn left and walk along the marsh. Briny tides rhythmically invade the branch, which flows into Little Mosquito Creek, which, in turn, empties into Mosquito Creek, which finally enters Chincoteague Bay. This little estuary contains a wide variety of plants. Those growing along the shore are able to tolerate brackish conditions created by the tides, but they occur here mainly because they are nourished by fresh water that seeps or runs off the surrounding slopes. Other plants growing near the center of the marsh are more salt tolerant and can withstand periodic immersions from the tides.

The path climbs and descends little knolls overlooking the lowland. The trail here is bordered with cut logs and branches and is easy to follow. Cross a gully on a wooden bridge and ascend slightly to arrive back at the trailhead.

Eastern Shore of Virginia National Wildlife Refuge

Explore Delmarva's newest refuge and help plan its future

Hiking distance: 1¼ miles
Hiking time: ¾ hour
Map: USGS Townsend

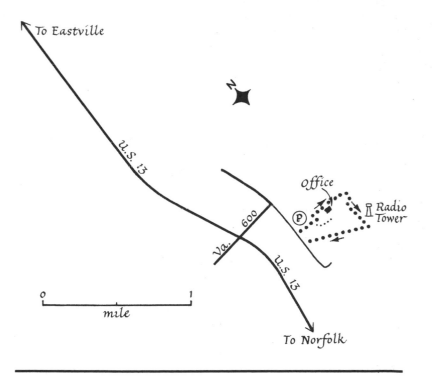

LYING NEAR THE SOUTHERN TIP OF THE DELMAR-
va Peninsula at Cape Charles, Eastern Shore of Virginia National
Wildlife Refuge was created to protect a critical resting and feeding
site for birds migrating along the Atlantic flyway. It presently occupies
about 180 acres, but more land is planned for acquisition.

Migratory birds tend to follow topographic features during their
long flights. In the autumn, southbound birds come down the Delmarva Peninsula by the millions, guided by the bordering bays and the
seacoast. As the peninsula narrows, it becomes a great, natural funnel.
When the birds reach land's end at Cape Charles, they face an arduous
nineteen-mile flight over the open waters of the Chesapeake Bay. Now
the weather becomes critical. If there is a strong northwest wind,
crossing the open water may be tragic since the wind could blow the
birds out to sea. At such times, those that attempt the crossing may
occasionally be seen beating their way back to shore, fighting the head
wind with their ebbing strength. When back on land, they are so
exhausted they can often be approached easily. Under such conditions,
few birds continue their migratory flight but, instead, stack up at the
cape to await better winds. When a front has brought in good weather,
the birds move through the cape in great numbers and head over the
Chesapeake with little hesitation.

Better-known and better-documented funnel phenomena occur during migratory seasons at Cape May, New Jersey, on the north shore
of Delaware Bay, and at Point Pelee, Ontario, on the north shore of
Lake Erie. Much remains to be learned about migrations at Cape
Charles, but it is clear it is used by large numbers of all sorts of birds
— shorebirds, ground birds, raptors, passerines, and waterfowl. Migrating monarch butterflies also probably depend upon the cape for rest
and food before starting over the bay. In addition, the area is home
to a rich assortment of winter, summer, and year-round avian residents.

Man has changed the environment of the cape in the past with little
regard for the birds or other wildlife. Military installations, like Fort
John Curtis and the Cape Charles Air Force Station, and major
thoroughfares, like the Chesapeake Bay Bridge-Tunnel, dominated
land use patterns in the area. The United States Fish and Wildlife
Service (USF&WS) took over the Cape Charles Air Force Station in
1984 and turned it into Cape Charles National Wildlife Refuge. The
name was changed to Eastern Shore of Virginia National Wildlife
Refuge in 1985.

The refuge does not look like a refuge; it looks like a mothballed military installation. But birds and other wildlife abound, and the USF&WS is drawing up plans to further enhance the area for use by birds. A diversity of habitats is being retained, ranging from groves of tall trees to expanses of short grass. Low, shrubby areas must be maintained for passerines, hunting grounds for raptors must be kept open, and ground birds such as bobwhite and woodcock must have places to feed and roam.

The refuge is still very much in its formative stages and advice and recommendations from the public are welcomed by the USF&WS. Help is especially needed in developing an accurate bird list. How many species of birds use the refuge, and in what numbers and in what seasons are they present? Also, what other animals are found on the refuge? Should the old air force buildings be torn down? What new roads and structures, if any, are needed? Should hiking trails or bicycle paths be built, and, if so, where? What new lands should be acquired? The refuge planners must consider a topographic inventory of the site, an analysis of soils, vegetation and forest types, animal life, drainage patterns, historic or archaeological sites, existing facilities, and means of access. Constraints will include development costs, budgetary and maintenance considerations, land prices, upkeep costs, and concerns and recommendations of local residents.

What do you think? Explore the refuge as it is now and then contact the refuge manager at R.D. 1, Box 122B, Cape Charles, Virginia, 23310, telephone 804-331-2760.

ACCESS

From the center of Eastville, drive south on U.S. Business 13 for 1.3 miles to U.S. 13, then continue south for another 14.0 miles to VA 600. Turn left and drive 0.3 mile to a "T" junction. Turn right to enter the refuge. Continue for another 0.3 mile and park in a paved area on the left, just before reaching a road to the left leading to the office.

TRAIL

Walk down the paved road toward the refuge office. The road may be blocked by a gate on weekends, but hikers are permitted. Fork left and then curve right, following the main road. The office appears on the right, at the edge of the old housing area of the air force station.

Continue through the now-deserted housing area, following the sidewalk. Curve to the right and come upon a high fence with a locked

173

gate separating the operations area of the former air force station from the housing area. Turn right and walk along the fence line, following it as it turns sharply to the left.

You will note inside the fence a tall, steel girder tower (painted in a red and white warning pattern) and a large, earthen bunker. At the old bunker, turn right, away from the fence, and walk along the unpaved runway (a very broad swath of closely mowed vegetation) of the former landing field. The airstrip is a good place to observe birds of open country, such as meadowlarks, savannah sparrows, and bobwhites. Raptors use this field as a hunting area, and vultures often circle overhead as they search for supper.

At the far end of the landing field, you will reach a paved road and must turn right to walk back to your car.

Chincoteague National Wildlife Refuge

A day hike on Assateague Island with good chances for close views of wildlife

Hiking distance: 13 miles
Hiking time: 6½ hours
Maps: USGS Chincoteague East; refuge map

ASSATEAGUE ISLAND LIES JUST OFF THE MAIN-
land of Maryland and Virginia. It is a long, narrow ribbon of sand,
stretching thirty-seven miles in a north-south direction, but is only
between one-fifth and three miles wide. Assateague is a textbook example of a barrier island, a physiographic feature occurring regularly
along the American coast from Massachusetts south to Texas. Although
common to the East Coast of the United States, barrier islands are
found only along less than 10 percent of all the earth's shorelines.

Islands like Assateague are believed to have been formed at the end
of or sometime after the last great Ice Age — perhaps 6,000 to 10,000
years ago. This part of North America was not glaciated, but the area
felt the influence of the ice far to the north. As the continental glaciers
melted, ocean waters rose, and mighty inland rivers carried great loads
of sediment that were deposited along the coast. The result was the
development of a broad continental shelf with shallow waters offshore.
Over the millenia, winds and tides combined with ocean waves to
create islands of fine sand near the mainland. Although thousands of
years old, Assateague is, geologically speaking, an infant. It can be
described as being storm built, for it is during severe ocean storms
that the great sculpting forces do most of their work. Most physiographic features, such as dunes, seen on Assateague are probably the
result of forces that occurred within a human lifespan. Even these
features can be very short-lived, since high winds and tides can change
the appearance of the island in just a day or two.

Born of the sea and continually shaped by it, the island seems more
related to the world of water than to that of land. It is an essential
part of that "ultimate wilderness that will never be tamed by men,"
as Jonathon Norton Leonard called the ocean. Protection for the wild
character of Assateague seems assured because almost the entire island
is preserved as public land. The Virginia portion was set aside as
Chincoteague National Wildlife Refuge in 1943. A few small islands
in the Maryland waters of Chincoteague Bay are also part of this refuge.

The island can be reached via bridges from the mainland. This easy
access, as well as the rewarding spectacle of animals (including Assateague's famous wild ponies) in natural habitats, makes Chincoteague
the second most visited national wildlife refuge in the country. Only
Merritt Island, Florida, records more annual visits, mainly because of
the people there to watch the rocket launches from nearby Cape Canav-
eral.

This day walk passes through marshland and stunted woodlands;

176

mosquitoes and other biting insects hungrily attack anything that offers a blood meal. Repellent is an absolute necessity for hikers during the warmer months. Dogs are not permitted on Chincoteague National Wildlife Refuge. A backpacking trek on Assateague Island is described in the next hike, where you will also find more information on the island and its history.

ACCESS

From Accomac, drive north on U.S. Business 13 for 2.0 miles. Continue north on U.S. 13 for 2.5 miles to VA 679, a country road that makes unexpected, unmarked turns. Turn right (north). In 10.2 miles (about 5.4 miles north of Modest Town), fork left. At a minor crossroads 1.0 mile north of Atlantic (13.6 miles from U.S. 13), turn left. Go another 1.4 miles to Wattsville and turn right (east) onto VA 175. Drive 7.8 miles to the town of Chincoteague on Chincoteague Island. Turn left (north) onto VA 175Y. In 0.4 mile, turn right onto VA 2113 (Maddox Boulevard). This road enters Chincoteague National Wildlife Refuge after 1.7 miles. Just 0.5 mile farther, turn left into the Refuge Visitor Center parking area. For this hike, park at the far side of the lot, away from the building and near our trail as it begins through the woods. The visitor center provides exhibits, maps, leaflets, information, restrooms, and drinking water.

TRAIL

Walk away from the visitor center on a boardwalk trail through the trees. (Avoid the paved bicycle path that exits the parking lot on the left.) You will shortly come upon paved Wildlife Drive — turn left. The drive is a four-mile loop through some of the most rewarding sections of the refuge; it is closed to cars until 3 p.m. each day so that hikers and bikers can enjoy the wildlife and scenery.

After slightly more than one-half mile, continue straight on an unpaved service road where Wildlife Drive curves to the right. Step around the gate to gain access to the service road. The road is open to hikers and is also used by official vehicles, including a "wildlife safari" trailer the refuge runs for the public. The program is conducted daily during the summer and on weekends in the spring and fall. Reservations are required and a fee is charged. The road is open to public vehicular traffic for about nine days each November in observance of National Wildlife Week.

177

Sika deer (actually a species of diminutive elk) were introduced onto Assateague Island from Japan many years ago. They now outnumber the native white-tailed deer.

The way passes through a pine forest, but the trees soon thin on the right, affording views of the upper reaches of Snow Goose Pool. This pond is one of seven such impoundments on the refuge, maintained to provide favored habitat and food plants for migrating waterfowl. The pools collect fresh water from rains but also can be inundated with salt water from the bay. Their depth and salinity are closely regulated, and some pools are lowered periodically. From October to March, the pools and marshes will likely be crowded with many species of ducks and geese, especially snow geese. These glistening white birds with black wing tips are perhaps directly responsible for establishing the refuge. Dwindling numbers of snow geese and other waterfowl alerted biologists to the necessity of providing feeding and resting areas for birds in the coastal marshes along their migratory routes.

You will soon come upon a side trail to the right that runs along the dike separating Snow Goose Pool and Mallard Marsh. Views across the marsh reach all the way to the dunes facing the Atlantic.

After about another one-half mile, another side trail goes to the right, following the dike that separates Mallard Marsh from Pintail Pool. In another mile, the road veers left and then right to pass around Gadwall Pool. Assateague Bay then comes into view on the left. Morris Island is the low, marshy island visible across the water. Behind it, the buildings on Chincoteague Island can be seen.

Pass through a gate with a corral on the left. The trail reaches Bow Beach on the bay side and turns to the left. Visible ahead and on the right are wash flats, favored gathering places for wildlife. Birds especially congregate on the great, level expanse of sand and shallow water. Waterfowl lounge on the sandy bars, wading birds stalk the pools, shorebirds and grackles walk and fly about, gulls soar by, and a peregrine falcon may come zooming out of the sky to snatch a duck from one of the flocks. Assateague is the best place in eastern North American to sight peregrine falcons. Although still rare, they are more numerous today due to a concerted reintroduction program that brought them back from the edge of extinction. Ponies will likely be seen here too, as well as perhaps a young raccoon wading through the water. Unlike their nocturnal parents, the less-cautious, youthful raccoons sometimes roam during the daylight hours.

The way leaves the wash flats for now and cuts through a pine forest for about three-fourths mile. Then the wash flats come into view on the seaward side once again. A road on a dike enters from the right across the flats about five miles into the hike. On the left of the trail in this area are the Smith Hammocks, a region of small sand dunes densely covered with shrubs and pines. Beyond the hammocks, the bay comes into view, reaching to the shoulder of the road at high tide.

At the north end of the wash flats, the trail veers slightly right and enters a forested area. It soon comes to a clearing where vehicles can turn around. Other paths lead off the circle to the northwest and northeast, but this spot marks the end of our trail; turn and walk back to your car.

To Berlin and
U.S. 113

U.S. 50

Md. 611

Md. 376

Ocean City Inlet

Sinepuxent Campsite
McCabe House

Seashore
Visitor
Center

Ⓟ

North Beach
North Beach
Ranger Station

Maryland

Chincoteague Bay

Little Levels
Campsite

Atlantic

State Line
Campsite

Ocean

Md.
Va.

Chincoteague
Island

Assateague
Island

Va.
175

Ⓟ

Toms Cove
Visitor Center

Toms
Cove

Chincoteague
Inlet

N

0   5   10
miles

Assateague Island

A four-day backpacking adventure by the sea

Hiking distance: 34½ miles
Hiking time: 4 days, 3 nights
Maps: USGS Tingles Island, Berlin,
  Ocean City, Whittington Point,
Boxiron, and Chincoteague East;
  national seashore map

ASSATEAGUE IS THE RICHEST AND LIVELIEST OF the Atlantic barrier islands. Created and dominated by the sea, the island is home to wild horses, to harmless reptiles like the terrestrial hog-nosed snake and the marine loggerhead turtle, and to aggressive (some say offensive) arthropods like ticks, sand flies, beach fleas, salt marsh mosquitoes, and biting flies such as greenheads and stable flies. Birds live here too — more than 275 species have been recorded. They include soaring turkey vultures, ten different kinds of hawks, including the rare and endangered peregrine falcon, bald eagles, and four species of owl. A wide array of thousands of wading birds, shorebirds, and waterfowl can be seen on Assateague. Loons, those symbols of wildness and far-off places, dive for fish in the winter surf. The American oystercatcher, the only bird of its kind in the eastern United States, uses its heavy, orange beak to pry between the hard shells of bivalves and dines on the meat within. Little birds like marsh wrens are more often heard than seen among the tall reeds of the marsh. Yellow-rumped warblers, unlike their insect-eating cousins, are found here even in winter because they feed on the clusters of light gray fruit from the bayberry. You can also find seaside sparrows, swallows, bobolinks, droves of red-winged blackbirds, and even tree-loving species like the brown-headed nuthatch who nests in the thick pine and oak forests near the southern end of the island.

There is also a nice variety of mammals on Assateague. In addition

181

to horses (by far the island's best known inhabitants), there are red foxes, raccoons, two different kinds of deer, opossums, muskrats, river otters, rabbits, Delmarva fox squirrels, and at least seven different species of marine mammals in the ocean off the island, often seen swimming through the water and sometimes found beached and dying on the sands. The sea casts up an amazing variety of creatures upon the strand: an array of shells, starfish, crabs, horseshoe crabs, sponges, jellyfish, sand dollars, shark teeth, whelk egg cases, fish — the list is almost endless. Assateague is blessed with many animals, some unusual, some unpleasant, but all — in their way — beautiful.

The island is one of the last along the Atlantic where the visitor can see a bit of nature in its pure state. All of Assateague, except for a few, scattered inholdings, is preserved by the federal government as a national seashore and a national wildlife refuge and by Maryland as a state park. Here, thick stands of beach grass create sand dunes and a place for other plants to gain a foothold. The hardy, seaside goldenrod colors the dunes with its golden flower plumes in late summer and early autumn. Seabeach evening primrose can be found trailing along the sand, its silvery white leaves covered with fine hairs that help retard evaporation of the plant's internal water supply. It has large, bright yellow blossoms that open in the late afternoon and close in the early morning.

The light seems a little more striking here than anywhere else in Delmarva — the sunrises, sunsets, the moon and stars a little more brilliant — and the air is almost always pure and clean. Cradling the island on all sides are the changing but eternal tides. After a day or so on Assateague, you become attuned to the motion of the planet and the universe. The celestial drama in the wide sky combines with the steady roar of the waves and the ceaseless wind to fill the air with the constantness of the elements in action.

Assateague is brushed by centuries of superstition, legend, and history, recently marked with heavy-handed attempts by man to forge a permanent presence, but the island remains a bastion of wildness, relatively undisturbed by the encroachments of civilization. We have few such places remaining in our ravaged, overcrowded world. Not many areas are better than the fastness of Assateague for a long walk under the sun, through the wind, by the sea.

Barrier island backpacking is an invigorating challenge, but careful planning and preparation are necessary for a successful, trouble-free trip. First, read the section on beach walking in the Introduction.

Since you will be out for four days, more attention must be given to specific details. This hike is not for the novice. I have seen even experienced backpackers falter and fail along the way. The insects, wind, and sun can combine to demoralize the unprepared hiker. Added to these discomforts is the physical effort of walking for miles through deep sand, especially when carrying a heavy pack. "Hiking five miles on Assateague is as strenuous as hiking ten or twelve miles in the mountains," a park ranger told me. Blisters, even on trail-hardened feet, are a common occurrence, so come equipped with adequate first-aid supplies.

The blazing sun is the first consideration; you cannot escape it. Sunburn or, worse, heatstroke and dehydration are backcountry emergencies that can be avoided by a sunscreen cream and adequate supplies of water. Sunglasses and a hat are added precautions to be included in your gear. No potable water is available in the backcountry; you must carry all water with you. The National Park Service suggests "a quart or more [water] for each day of the trip" on the leaflet they hand out to backpackers. This quantity is perhaps low. Other outdoor experts recommend two quarts of water daily for adults under normal conditions and up to four quarts for heavy activity. A friend and I carried about 2½ quarts of water per person per day on this hike (in relatively cool weather in April); we had very little left. Some Assateague backpackers carry canned foods instead of freeze-dried foods that require water for cooking.

The wind is constant and sometimes very strong. It blows sand into your boots, tent, stove, and food. Tent pegs work loose under the tugging of the gusts. To prevent a tent from collapsing on top of you in the middle of the night, use special pegs designed to anchor in soft sand. I make my own pegs out of one-quarter-inch wooden dowels, cut fifteen inches long and notched to hold the guy ropes. I drive the entire peg into the sand and use a small, plastic trowel to dig it out when breaking camp. Pack a couple of extra pegs in case they break or get lost in the sand drifts. Even hot, summer days can turn into cool, breezy nights, so a windbreaker is a necessary addition.

Backpackers must be armored against the legions of blood-sucking insects inhabiting the island. The voracious feeding of salt marsh mosquitoes must be experienced to be appreciated, but they are usually discouraged by repellents. Staying on the beach is another fairly successful way to avoid most of the mosquitoes, because they are deterred by the strong winds. The wild ponies have learned this trick and often

183

spend their time on the beach. High winds generally do not stop the strong-flying greenheads. These are big insects that bite painfully; most repellents seem ineffective against them. Greenhead season on the island leads you to appreciate the night, since these insects fly only during the day.

Because of the biting insects, some backpackers plan their trips for early spring or late fall when insects are not on the wing. Indeed, the time of year should be a major consideration as you plan your hike. Summer brings the most visitors to the island, especially on warm weekends and holidays. Despite the crowds, however, the backcountry is often mostly deserted. After June and well into September, the ocean is warm enough for swimming. Prior to May and after the first killing frost in autumn, insects are no longer a nuisance, the weather is often mild, and there are fewer people. Winter backpacking along the ocean can be severe and requires special knowledge and equipment. Whatever the season, be prepared for sudden and dramatic shifts in weather. I recall one hike along the shore in August when the skies became overcast and a howling, onshore wind drove salt spray up the beach all the way to the front dune. The moisture and wind combined to create very chilly conditions that could have led to hypothermia in unwary hikers. During extremely adverse weather, such as hurricanes and northeasters, the hike should not be attempted. Adequate warning of these major storms is usually provided by weather forecasts. Locally severe thunderstorms with lightning pose special problems since you are the highest object on the beach. Seek shelter among the dunes and wait out the storm.

One of the lingering memories of your trip will be the fragrance of burning driftwood in your campfire or cooking fire. However, adequate supplies of driftwood for cooking are by no means assured, so you need to carry a small, lightweight stove with enough fuel for four days. A windscreen and hurricane matches that do not snuff out in the wind should be included.

The National Park Service maintains three backcountry campsites for the exclusive use of overnight hikers. The sites are near the ocean, behind the primary dune. This chapter describes a hike along the length of the island using these three designated campsites. Four additional areas set up for canoe camping can also be used by backpackers; all these latter campsites are on the bayside. Small signs along the beach and along the back road plainly point the way to the campsites. The three areas along the oceanside are open year-round, but the four sites on the bayside are closed during waterfowl season. All seven areas are in Maryland. Each site is equipped with a picnic table and a chemical toilet. Camping elsewhere in the backcountry is prohibited. A parking and backcountry permit must be obtained in person before you start your trip; permits are available at either the Seashore or Toms Cove visitor centers or at the North Beach Ranger Station.

A young hiker tests her speed against incoming breakers on Assateague Island.

Part of the island traversed by the walk is also used by off-road vehicles (ORVs). Be alert for vehicles approaching from behind while walking on the beach. Sometimes the sound of the surf drowns out engine noise. A long, day hike in the refuge portion of Assateague is described in the previous chapter, which includes comments on the island's formation and geology.

ACCESS

This hike requires two vehicles. To drop off the first car, drive south from Snow Hill on MD 12 for 12.2 miles to the Virginia line. There the highway becomes VA 679. Continue south for another 7.6 miles to Wattsville and VA 175. Turn left (east) and go 7.8 miles to the town of Chincoteague on Chincoteague Island. Turn left (north) onto VA 175Y. In 0.4 mile, turn right onto VA 2113 (Maddox Boulevard). This road goes straight across Assateague Channel, entering Assateague Island National Seashore and Chincoteague National Wildlife Refuge after 1.7 miles. Continue driving down this road (here known as Beach Road) for 3.0 miles until you come upon a small traffic circle. Take the leftmost road off the circle and enter parking area 1. Toms Cove Visitor Center is on the right. Leave one of the cars at the far northern end of the lot.

If coming from Accomac, go north on U.S. Business 13 for 2.0 miles, and then continue north on U.S. 13 for 2.5 miles to VA 679. Turn right (north) and be alert, because this country road makes unmarked turns. In 10.2 miles (about 5.4 miles north of Modest Town), keep left at a fork. At a minor crossroads 1.0 mile north of Atlantic (13.6 miles from U.S. 13), turn left. Drive another 1.4 miles to Wattsville and turn right onto VA 175. Follow the above directions to Assateague Island.

Having parked a car at the Toms Cove Visitor Center, drive the other vehicle back to Wattsville and turn right (north) on VA 679. Enter Maryland and continue north on MD 12 for 10.5 miles to U.S. 113. Turn right (north). Drive 15.6 miles to MD 376 in Berlin and turn right (east). This highway ends at MD 611 after 4.0 miles; turn right (south). You will pass the Seashore Visitor Center on the right after 3.0 miles. Just beyond, cross Sinepuxent Bay on the Verrazzano Bridge (named for the first white explorer in these waters) and arrive at Assateague. When on the island, turn right at the first opportunity and drive for another 2.5 miles, bearing right at a fork. The roads you see to the left lead into Assateague State Park. Beyond the state land, the road becomes North Beach Drive. Turn left into the North Beach parking lot. A few parking spaces, near the North Beach Ranger Station and marked by signs that read "Hike-in Campsite Parking Only," are reserved for you.

DAY 1
North Beach to Sinepuxent
Hiking distance: 4½ miles
Hiking time: 3 hours

Follow one of the walkways across the dunes and turn left (north) along the ocean. North Beach is a major national park recreation area, featuring camping, picnicking, and swimming. Enter Assateague State Park after one-half mile. Backpackers must stay on the beach through state land; use of the park's facilities, such as showers, water fountains, store, and campground is prohibited.

North of the state park, you will reenter the national seashore and will walk along an isolated and secluded beach. ORVs are not permitted, and soon you seemingly have the whole island to yourself. In this untamed north end, we saw our first wild ponies — two of them, standing near the top of the front dune. They turned and wandered away slowly as we grew near. Assateague's horses were always said to have been descended from Spanish horses that swam ashore after an ancient galleon cracked up in an ocean storm, but the tales were always considered mostly legend, with no proof and little credibility. Recent research, however, confirms the old stories and proves with little doubt that horses reached Assateague as a result of a Spanish shipwreck. The new evidence is even more intriguing than the old legends.

In the early 1800s, the armed merchantman *San Lorenzo* was beating north along the American coast, bound for Spain and carrying a rich cargo of gold and silver from Spain's Peruvian colony. Also on board were about one hundred small horses — draft animals used by the Spaniards in the Panamanian mines. Purposefully bred to be small so they could be lowered into narrow shafts and could work in the close confines of mine tunnels, the horses were also blind. Kept permanently underground in darkness and in lifelong servitude, they were blinded by the Spaniards so they could be more easily handled. Indian rebels in Panama had forced the closure of some mines, and these horses

187

were being moved back to the old country to continue their subterranean work.

Off of Assateague, the *San Lorenzo* broke up in a heavy gale and ran aground. Some of the horses escaped from the flooding hold and somehow got to the island through the stormy surf — to freedom. Facing overwhelming odds, they managed to survive, reproduce, and establish a wild herd of free-roaming offspring.

The story of the wreck was told to a Spanish tribunal in 1821 by Don Pedro Murphy, a Cuban navigator and possibly the only human survivor. Don Pedro and a companion also made it to the beach. Shipwrecked on a deserted shore, they began to walk northward, likely following the same route as part of our hike. The companion died near Cape Henlopen, but Don Pedro was rescued by fishermen. He made his way by boat to Philadelphia and eventually to Spain. His testimony at the tribunal states that some horses reached the shore. Later evidence was added by an American fishing rights commissioner who inspected Assateague in 1826. He reported finding forty-five tiny horses, many blind; there had been none on the island during a visit nine years earlier. The ponies are believed to have reached their present size (smaller than a standard horse and larger than a Shetland pony) by interbreeding with other horses moved to the island by mainland farmers; Assateague was used as an open range for livestock grazing by the early settlers in the area.

You will eventually pass the white, rambling McCabe House, built in 1949 by the former chairman of the board of the Scott Paper Company as an ocean retreat. It is now used by the National Park Service to board seasonal employees and visiting scientists. The caretaker's quarters and boat dock are behind the house on the bayside. McCabe built his home well back from the primary dune, but now sand is drifting onto the front porch and it seems only a matter of time before the structure will be reclaimed by the island's natural forces. The plight of the old McCabe House dramatically illustrates the rapid westward erosion of the entire north end of Assateague. The island has moved more than one thousand feet to the west in the last thirty years, primarily because jetties were constructed to keep the Ocean City Inlet open, thereby depriving the north end of sand needed to replace that lost in beach erosion.

About three-fourths mile north of the house, you will reach Sinepuxent Campsite. The camp is located at a very narrow portion of the island, and both sunsets over Sinepuxent Bay and sunrises over the

188

Atlantic Ocean can be enjoyed from your tent. Wildlife is abundant. Towhees, warblers, and other small birds flit about the thickets surrounding the camp. We saw muskrats swimming in the bay marshes, and, in the far distance, a stallion drove his small herd of mares and foals over the brow of the dune onto the beach. Driftwood littered the area.

From Sinepuxent, the individual street and shop lights of Ocean City are plainly visible on the northern horizon. The city glitters softly, five miles across and away. From this distance, the city is as inaudible as it is beautiful; except for the dull, distant clamor of the surf, all is quiet. Here, you can feel utterly removed from the throngs of the city and the cares of civilization. Although man's current presence is within sight, you are surrounded by an immense solitude created by the spare, sudden beauty of the land and the vastness of the North Atlantic.

As the night grows cooler, you may want to draw closer to your fire and think of other, earlier visitors to these shores. The saga of Colonel Henry Norwood, whose tale remains one of the heroic survival epics of Assateague, occurred near this camp. In *A Voyage to Virginia* Norwood told how the *Virginia Merchant,* the ship on which he was a passenger, became ensnared in a mighty winter storm in January 1650. The vessel was sailing from England to Virginia by way of the West Indies but was blown off course to near northern Assateague Island. In a battered ship, with water and food running out, the crew and passengers were near despair. Norwood gained permission from the captain to lead a shore party of nineteen men and women in search of fresh water, food, and a safe harbor for making repairs in the damaged ship. Once on the island, they were able to shoot a duck, gather some oysters, and find water. They spent the night ashore, rendering "thanks to almighty God for opening this door of deliverance." Their joy was short-lived, however, for at daybreak they discovered the *Virginia Merchant* under full sail far out to sea, heading south. Norwood wrote: "In this amazement and confusion of mind that no words can express, did our miserable distress'd party console with each other our being so crully abandon'd and left to the last despairs of human help, or indeed of ever seeing more the face of man."

Norwood assumed command of the group, sending some to search for Indians, others to hunt ducks and geese, a group to gather wood, and the rest to construct shelters. "In quartering our family we did observe the decency of distinguishing sexes: we made a small hut for the poor weak women to be by themselves; our cabin for men was of

189

the same fashion, but much more spacious, as our numbers were."

The castaways' lot soon became desperate as the island became a deadly trap. Waterfowl were driven away by strong winds, and one bird they managed to shoot was stolen by wolves. High tides made it difficult to harvest enough oysters. They subsisted by boiling "a sort of weed" ("the only green...that the island afforded") with their few oysters. Renewed storms drove across the island, weakening the party to the point where it was all they could do to get wood for the fires. Starving and frozen, the little band found it an ordeal merely to ward off death. Norwood wrote:

> Of the three weak women...one had the envied happiness to die about this time; and it was my advice to the survivors, who were following her apace, to endeavour their own preservation by converting her dead carcase into food, as they did to good effect. The same counsel was embrac'd by those of our sex: the living fed upon the dead; four of our company having the happiness to end their miserable lives on Sunday night....Their chief distemper, 'tis true, was hunger; but it pleased God to hasten their exit by an immoderate access of cold, caused by a most terrible storm of hail and snow at northwest,...which did not only dispatch those four to their long homes, but did sorely threaten all that remained alive, to perish by the same fate.

Just when all seemed lost, a small group of Assateague Indians found the party and shared their food with them. The Assateagues rescued Norwood and the other survivors by transporting them to the mainland and then escorting them south to Indian villages on Virginia's Eastern Shore. Norwood eventually got to Jamestown and, subsequently, returned to Europe. He closed his account with an acknowledgement to "the good providence of a gracious God, who helpeth us in our low estate, and causeth his angels to pitch tents round about them that trust in him."

DAY 2
Sinepuxent to Little Levels, Via North Beach
Hiking distance: 9 miles
Hiking time: 6 hours

Retrace your path 4½ miles to North Beach. Here you can dump the trash you packed out and load up with fresh water and supplies for the next three days.

You may want to make North Beach a welcome lunch break. Around the turn of the century there was a small settlement here. The community of North Beach consisted only of a few houses, a one-room school, a saltworks, and a lifesaving station. The station was manned by hardy men who worked for the United States Life Saving Service, a forerunner of the Coast Guard. Equipped and trained to rescue shipwrecked mariners and to assist in salvaging stranded vessels, the surfmen, as they were called, risked their lives in the pounding gales and battering surf. The North Beach station was operational from 1884 to 1954, first under the Life Saving Service and later under the Coast Guard.

When you are repacked, continue south along the shore. Beyond the swimming area, ORVs use the beach and the rough road running behind the dunes. This road, now called the ORV Access Road by the National Park Service, was known as Baltimore Avenue in the 1950s when Ocean Beach Corporation owned most of the Maryland portion of the island. Other developers had been at work on Assateague, but Ocean Beach brought sophisticated techniques and massive capital to develop the island systematically by dividing the land into small lot offerings. They mounted an aggressive sales campaign that included large-scale advertising, colorful promotion, and personal contacts by representatives. By 1962, the company had sold 5,850 lots, had paved Baltimore Avenue and other roads, had installed electric lines, and were moving toward establishment of hotels, shopping centers, and sewer lines.

Early that year, a severe winter storm struck the island, completely demolishing most of the houses that had been built. It was the most destructive storm thus far this century, exceeding in fury even the hurricanes that sometimes batter the coast. The North Atlantic, driven ashore by high winds and tides, surged across the island all the way to the bay at several points. The electric lines snapped, and Baltimore Avenue was washed away in most places. Remnants of broken and crumbling asphalt can still be found along the old roadway or scattered among the dunes. It is now a road to nowhere, waiting to completely disappear with the next storm or to be buried under sand.

After the water subsided and the immensity of the loss was assessed, Ocean Beach and other private interests petitioned the federal government to engineer protection for the island from natural forces. Studies showed that the cost would be prohibitive, so the request for federal

191

assistance was denied. The great storm stilled private land speculation long enough to permit establishment of Assateague Island National Seashore in 1965.

Little Levels, your campsite for the night, is 4½ miles from North Beach. It lies at a fairly wide part of the island, with extensive wash flats occurring bayward of the camp. On our trip, the sun was nearing the horizon as we scoured the flats for firewood, and a red fox loped across the barren expanse, starting on his nightly hunt.

DAY 3
Little Levels to State Line
Hiking distance: 8 miles
Hiking time: 5 hours

You will almost certainly encounter surf fishermen on the Maryland portion of Assateague at all times of the year. They drive into the backcountry in their ORVs and cast baited lines into the ocean in quest of black drum, striped bass, flounder, white perch, bluefish, and many others.

In the autumn you may also see hunters (mainly on the bayside) because Assateague Island is one of the few national parks that allows hunting and trapping. Congress specifically included hunting as a recreational use of the seashore when it was established. Sportsmen rush to the island during legal seasons, going after white-tailed deer, Sika deer, mourning doves, rails, woodcocks, snipe, gallinules, Canada geese, snow geese, brant, scaups, scoters, eiders, old squaw, mallards, black ducks, wood ducks, hooded mergansers, mottled ducks, blue-winged teal, green-winged teal, pintails, gadwalls, shovelers, coots, and other animals.

State Line, your last campsite of the trek, is nestled among the dunes about one mile north of the Maryland–Virginia border. Night-time at State Line can be immense, grand, and mysterious under a starlit sky. The island evokes a sense of isolation far removed in distance and time from mainland activity. At dusk, the rotating beacon of the Assateague light (more than eleven miles away) comes into view, sweeping across the heavens in a soft, diffuse arc. The lighthouse, built in 1867, is near the southern end of the island; its 800,000-candle power-rated light can be seen for nineteen nautical miles, warning ships of the treacherous shoals that lie just offshore.

At certain times of the year, light from an entirely different source

192

also can be seen at night on the beach. Waves crashing onto the shore flash with an eerie, greenish light just as the top breaks into foam. Sometimes the entire face of a long breaker will light up in sequence, resembling a dancing chain reaction down the beach. The strange, fiery light is caused by billions of tiny phosphorescent protozoa, part of the rich pelagic life of the sea. Countless numbers of these minute creatures are cast onto the beach with every wave. When you walk across wet sand at low tide, the protozoa luminesce in sparkling, radiating, star-shaped bursts of cold light. Tracing patterns in the sand with your fingers has the same result — I felt like a wizard with magic beams of light at my fingertips. These animals evidently shine when they are excited by being tossed by waves, jarred by a footfall, joggled by a finger, or perhaps stimulated by their neighbors. The protozoa glow softly and ghostlike for a few moments as they cling to your wet, sandy skin.

The beach at night is alive with many other creatures. Small phosphorescent shrimp can also be found along the swash marks. Farther up the beach, on drier sand, your flashlight beam will likely intercept ghost crabs. Living in damp burrows in the sand by day, these small crabs emerge in great numbers at night to scavenge the beach and to soak in the surf. Although essentially terrestrial, they retain a close link to the sea, returning by necessity to the water to wet their gills and to lay eggs. Young ghost crabs reveal their marine ancestry by becoming part of the open ocean plankton. Although a ghost crab will remain momentarily immobilized by your flashlight beam, they soon dart away so quickly it is impossible to track them. Their protective coloration and lightning swiftness enable them to seemingly vanish.

DAY 4
State Line to Toms Cove
Hiking distance: 13 miles
Hiking time: 8½ hours

Assateague has saved its best and most dramatic beach for the last day. Our hike continues south for about one mile and enters Virginia and Chincoteague National Wildlife Refuge. This maritime wilderness in Virginia brings to mind the words of Thoreau who, writing of the beach on Cape Cod in another century, said: "The solitude was that of the ocean and desert combined."

A fence bisects the island at the border. It keeps the pony herds of

193

the two states separate (the Virginia horses are owned by the Chincoteague Volunteer Fire Department and are rounded up each year) and also prevents ORVs from crossing into Virginia. No vehicles are permitted for the next twelve miles.

The wild, lonely shore is a beachcomber's paradise. We could not resist adding slightly to the weight of our packs by collecting many of the shells we came across. Shells recently washed ashore were near the surf, still gleaming with moisture, while high on the beach a long windrow of flotsam yielded other relics. In just a short distance, we found scallops, coquinas, slipper and jingle shells, and many others. Successful shell collecting is dependent upon the slope and shape of the beach, ocean currents, presence or absence of offshore sand bars, and proper timing. The best time for finding shells and other remains cast ashore is when the tide is out. Extra low tides occur immediately after a new or full moon.

When we were about a mile north of Toms Cove, we saw two horseshoe crabs washing ashore ahead of us. Since it was spring, with night coming on, they were almost certainly coming in on a high tide to mate and lay eggs; the smaller male was clinging to the back of the much larger female.

We stopped to watch. If all went well, the female would hollow out a small depression in the sand just below the average high-water mark and would lay her eggs. The accompanying male would then deposit sperm on top of them. But a particularly rough breaker caught the animals, breaking the male's hold, and sent them both tumbling up the beach. The male was lucky enough to catch the retreating wave and ride it back into the sea, quickly disappearing under the dark water. The gravid female was thrown higher and landed upside down, her ten legs splaying skyward and grasping only air. Now she was in danger either of being stranded by the tide and left to dry out or of being eaten by gulls at dawn. I removed my pack for more agility and scooped up the heavy female by resting her hard, dorsal carapace in the palm of my hand. I inched towards the sea, trying to get as close as possible without getting doused. As a big wave surged landward, I gave a long heave, sending the horseshoe crab out as far as I could. She landed upside down with a big splash, righted herself in the water, and dove. An increasing wind from an approaching storm was blowing offshore, and that breeze, combined with a local current, might give her another chance.

I retrieved my pack and finished the last mile, soaked from my

194

knees down. We were guided through the deepening dark, like mariners at sea, by the Assateague light. As we walked, I reflected that saving one female horseshoe crab did not really much matter to the preservation of the species as a whole — they are one of the most common and successful marine animals along the Atlantic Coast. So vast are their numbers, that the loss of a single female is infinitesimal. But it made a difference to that one individual.

Guidebooks from Backcountry Publications

Written for people of all ages and experience, these popular and carefully prepared books feature detailed trail and tour directions, notes on points of interest and natural phenomena, maps and photographs.

WALKS AND RAMBLES SERIES

Walks and Rambles Delmarva, by Jay Abercrombie $8.95

Walks and Rambles Westchester (NY) and Fairfield (CT) Counties (available Spring 1986)

Walks and Rambles Rhode Island (available Spring 1986)

25 Walks in the Dartmouth-Lake Sunapee Region, by Mary L. Kibling $4.95

BIKING SERIES

25 Bicycle Tours in Vermont, by John Freidin $7.95

25 Bicycle Tours in New Hampshire, by Tom and Susan Heavey $6.95

25 Bicycle Tours in the Finger Lakes, by Mark Roth and Sally Waters $6.95

25 Bicycle Tours in and around New York City, by Dan Carlinsky and David Heim $6.95

25 Bicycle Tours in Eastern Pennsylvania, by Dale Adams and Dale Speicher $6.95

CANOEING SERIES

Canoe Camping Vermont and New Hampshire Rivers, by Roioli Schweiker $6.95

Canoeing Central New York, by William P. Ehling $8.95

Canoeing Massachusetts, Rhode Island and Connecticut, by Ken Weber $6.95

HIKING SERIES

Discover the Adirondacks 1 (revised edition available Spring 1986)

Discover the Adirondacks 2, by Barbara McMartin $7.95

50 Hikes in the Adirondacks, by Barbara McMartin $8.95

50 Hikes in Central New York, by William P. Ehling $8.95

50 Hikes in the Hudson Valley, by Barbara McMartin and Peter Kick $9.95

50 Hikes in Central Pennsylvania, by Tom Thwaites $9.95

50 Hikes in Eastern Pennsylvania, by Carolyn Hoffman $8.95

50 Hikes in Western Pennsylvania, by Tom Thwaites $8.95

50 Hikes in Maine, by John Gibson $8.95

50 Hikes in the White Mountains, by Daniel Doan $8.95

50 More Hikes in New Hampshire, by Daniel Doan $8.95

50 Hikes in Vermont, 3rd edition, revised by the Green Mountain Club $8.95

50 Hikes in Massachusetts, by John Brady and Brian White $8.95

50 Hikes in Connecticut, by Gerry and Sue Hardy $8.95

50 Hikes in West Virginia (available Spring 1986)

The above titles are available at bookstores and at certain sporting goods stores or may be ordered directly from the publisher. For complete descriptions of these and other guides, write: Backcountry Publications, P.O. Box 175, Woodstock, VT 05091.